OF SACRAMENTS AND SACRIFICE

By
Reverend Clifford Howell, S.J.

Discussion Questions by
Reverend Alexius Portz, O.S.B.

THE LITURGICAL PRESS

St. John's Abbey   Collegeville, Minnesota

NIHIL OBSTAT

Ioannes Eidenschink, O.S.B., J.C.D.
Censor Deputatus

IMPRIMI POTEST

Daniel H. Conway, S.J.
Provincialis
Missourii Provinciae

✠ Balduinus Dworschak, O.S.B.
Abbas
Sancti Ioannis Baptistae

IMPRIMATUR

✠ Petrus W. Bartholome, D.D.
Coadiutor Episcopus
Sancti Clodoaldi

Die 29a octobris, 1952

Tenth printing—*Thirty thousand*
Copyright 1952
The Order of St. Benedict, Inc.
Collegeville, Minnesota

PREFACE

"THE WORK of our redemption is continued, and its fruits are imparted to us during the celebration of the liturgy," says Pope Pius XII in his encyclical *Mediator Dei* (n. 29 NCWC edition). In this book will be found some account of the work of our redemption precisely under this aspect of its continuation and application through the liturgy. The first part deals with some underlying principles and with the seven sacraments; the second part treats of "the crowning act of the sacred liturgy" (n. 49), namely, the sacrifice of the Mass.

All these chapters originally appeared in the liturgical review *Orate Fratres* (now published under its new name of *Worship*). The Editor wanted some articles which would be intelligible to new readers of the review—readers who had as yet no "liturgical background," and he did me the great honor of asking me to write the series which, it was hoped, would help not only beginners but also others who desire to spread the knowledge of the liturgy. The articles are collected here almost exactly as they were first published; a few minor changes and the addition of one or two small connecting passages are the only differences in the text.

But an important addition comes into the book in the form of the illustrations. These have been drawn by Miss Jane Sampson who has put into artistic form the ideas supplied to her. My best thanks are due to her for her fine work, and to the Editor for his gracious permission to republish material from his excellent review which I heartily commend as a "follow up" to this book.

CLIFFORD HOWELL, S.J.

CONTENTS

PART ONE OF SACRAMENTS

    Why Worship? 3
    The Good Tidings 12
    Sharing Divine Life 23
    Of Things Visible and Invisible 34
    The Making of a Christian 46
    Increase of the Body 57
    Holy Orders 69
    The Health of the Mystical Body 78

PART TWO OF SACRIFICE

    The Meaning of Sacrifice 93
    Man's Yearning 105
    What Happens at Mass 116
    Completing the Sacrifice 128
    The Mass is a Liturgy 139
    Problems of Participation 151
    A Glance into the Past 160
    Liturgical Piety 173

PART ONE
OF SACRAMENTS

A drawing after the fresco in the Church of St. Joseph, Easton, Pennsylvania.

The Blessed Trinity (triangle) is the source of all grace—or divine life—which comes to us through the One Mediator, Christ, triumphant upon His Cross. From Calvary there gush forth the seven streams of grace (the Sacraments) to refresh the whole world. The faithful are represented by the two harts who look up to our Saviour in gratitude after slaking their thirst at the fountains of living water. The Psalmist says that "the just shall flourish like palm trees"; and so the palms here represent those who are growing in grace.

CHAPTER ONE

WHY WORSHIP?

IF THE AVERAGE Man reads some advertisement which says that a certain car has a body designed on a kecharitomenous principle, with a holosphuretic radiator in front, an anaskeuazic boot behind and a skiatrophic roof on top, he forthwith rushes off brandishing a check book in one hand and a fountain pen in the other to place an immediate order with the nearest distributing agency. (If this is not so, why do car advertisements abound in mysterious words of this type?)

Yet if the Average Catholic picks up some book or a periodical such as *Worship* or *Liturgy,* and reads on its inside cover that it is "devoted to the liturgical apostolate," he promptly puts it down again. If it said that it dealt with Theopneustic Euchology (which, as a matter of fact, it does) he would not merely put it down, but would drop it as if it were red hot.

Why do strange long words attract him if printed in *Automobile Facts* but repel him if printed in *Worship?* Surely because he is interested in the subject dealt with by *Automobile Facts* but not interested in the subject dealt with by *Worship.* The Average Man doesn't know what "anaskeuazic" means; but he realizes it has something to do with cars. And he is *interested in cars.* The word makes him feel there is something

The picture. Mankind is represented by the male and female figures; the angels are as described by the Prophet Isaias; all are adoring God, whose unity of nature is represented by the circle (a figure without beginning or end), and whose trinity of persons is indicated by the triangle.

about the advertised car which he doesn't know. And, because of his interest in cars, he isn't happy till he has found out what it is. When the Average Catholic sees a word like "liturgical" he also doesn't know what it means. But he feels no compelling urge to find out because he doesn't even realize what it has to do *with*. It does not, so far as he is aware, have anything to do with anything which has to do with him. And so the Average Catholic is not interested! And he doesn't read *Worship*.

And that is where he is wrong. He is just about as wrong as he could be! For the word "liturgical" has to do with *worship*. Precisely what it has to do with worship we shall see later. The point at issue now is that worship is far more important than motor cars. Not everybody is concerned with cars. It is possible in some circumstances to lead an entirely satisfactory life while having nothing to do with cars. But it is not possible in any circumstances whatever to lead a satisfactory life while having nothing to do with worship.

Cars concern some people: worship concerns everybody. If some people are interested in cars, everybody ought to be interested in worship. With cars we "go places" in this world: and it is usually possible to get there by alternative means such as trains or horses. But with worship we reach our goal in the next world, and there are no means whatever alternative to worship. And we aren't bound to go anywhere in this world, but we are all bound to go somewhere in the next world. Which all goes to show that the subject of worship is vastly more important than the subject of motor cars.

Let us start, then, by trying to see what it is all about. If we begin from the fact that man is God's creature, we see that man must take due notice of that fact and behave accordingly. But already we are dealing with the very elements of "religion." That, after all, is what religion amounts to: "taking due notice of God and behaving accordingly."

You will notice that there are two elements here: (a) "taking due notice of God" (which is what we call worship) and (b) "behaving accordingly" (which is what we call morals). The peculiar thing is that one sometimes finds people who seem to be doing (b) without doing (a); while others look as if they are doing (a) without being particularly shining examples of (b)! Yet obviously (a), if done properly, could hardly help producing (b).

Let us first have a look at those people who seem to be "behaving accordingly" even though they do not "take due notice of God." They are the people who say they don't go in for any religion, yet on the whole they are decent to their fellow men, they "do nobody any harm," they are generous, truthful, loyal, brave . . . they do a whole lot of things which, as a matter of fact, God does want them to do. Such naturally good people are not unknown—I expect we all know somebody like that. Yet does their behavior make sense? Is it really enough to be as they are?

Surely not! For they are like children who are pleasant with brothers and sisters and schoolmates, who work well at school and get good marks, who in fact, do all sorts of things which their father wants them to do. But they take no notice of their father. True, they refrain from kicking him on the shins, or emptying tins of used sump oil into his bed, or sprinkling powdered glass into his dinner. They don't do anything against their father. But they just leave him alone. They do not "take due notice" of him; they never talk to him or thank him or praise him; they just ignore him. Would he regard them as satisfactory children? No! Then neither would God regard as satisfactory creatures men who, even though well-behaved, just ignore Him and take no notice of Him whatever.

Now let us look at the people who seem to "take due notice of God" by worshiping Him, and yet do not "behave accordingly." Again I expect we all know somebody like that: somebody who goes to church, yet won't pay a decent wage to his employees (or won't do an honest day's work for his employer); somebody who says his prayers, yet is notorious for his venomous and lying tongue. Their behavior also doesn't make sense. They are like children who talk to their father, praise him, thank him for all he has done, "take due notice of him" in fact; and yet they don't do what he wants; they play truant from school, throw stones at the windows of his house, pour sand into his car's gas tank. Will their father regard them as satisfactory children? No! Then neither would God regard as satisfactory creatures men who, though they seem to "take due notice of Him" by worship, do not "behave accordingly" by doing what He wants. What is wanted is both elements of religion: there must be worship *and* behavior.

Yet I think everybody will agree that, of the two, worship is more fundamental. If worship is genuine and sincere it *must* produce good behavior. If children genuinely love their father and are sincere when they praise him and thank him for all he does for them, they cannot fail to do the things which please him. So also if men are fully conscious of what they are doing when they worship God, and if they really mean what they say in their prayers, then they are sure to lead lives pleasing to God.

We conclude, then, that good behavior does not always lead to good worship; whereas good worship must always lead to good behavior. (If it does not, it is not good worship but sham worship.) To express the same thing in a slightly different way: if only men will worship God properly (which means intelligently and sincerely) they will behave themselves. When they behave badly it is either because they worship badly (unintelligently or insincerely) or else they don't worship God at all. Hence there is nothing more important in the whole world than that men should worship God properly—in sincerity and in truth.

Everybody will agree that at present the world is in a perfectly shocking state. There is no end of cruelty, tyranny, hatred, injustice, dishonesty, lust, jealousy, selfishness, cynicism, hypocrisy and every other vice one could name. And these are not merely impersonal evils. It means that some individual man or men are being cruel, some specific persons are acting as tyrants, some definite human beings are hating or swindling or lusting or whatever it may be. And in every single case it is true that they are not "taking due notice of God"—they are not worshiping God, in sincerity and in truth. That neglect of God is the basic evil of which all the other evils are but a symptom. Getting rid of symptoms never cures a disease. One must eliminate the root-cause.

Hence it is not enough to campaign against all these vices. The only cure is to eliminate godlessness. Those who are, as a matter of fact, creatures of God are ignoring the fact that God is their Master. In proportion as they come to recognize this—in proportion as they worship God—so will the lot of mankind, even here below, improve. That is why there is nothing so important in the whole world as that men should worship God in sincerity and in truth.

"That's all very well," you may say, "but what has it got to do with me? I can't make the whole world worship God properly." No, you can't. But you can help. You can look to your own worship. I have no doubt that as a Catholic you do a fair amount of worshiping. You come to Mass on Sundays; you say your daily prayers; maybe you do even more than that.

Fine! But what of the effect? Does it overflow into your daily life? Does it really make you behave better than the fellow next door who, as a non-Catholic, doesn't go to Mass and perhaps says no prayers yet seems a decent enough chap? For it should! If he, who takes no notice of his Father in heaven (I'm not blaming him—perhaps he knows no better) nevertheless behaves himself well, then surely you who profess to know and love your Father who is in heaven ought to be behaving yourself still better!

We Catholics *ought* to be noticeably better people than those outside the Church. We ought to be quite outstanding for our charity, justice, truthfulness, generosity, purity, unselfishness, honesty and all the other virtues. Some are or have been: and those are the saints (both the canonized and uncanonized). But not all of us are like that. Yet we *should* be. "Be ye holy as your heavenly Father is holy!" said our Lord. "This is the will of God," said St. Paul, "your sanctification!"

So we *ought* to be saints! Then why aren't we, in spite of the fact that we do our worshiping?

The answer is surely that when the saints worshiped God it was no mere external performance. It *meant* everything to them. But when some of us worship, it amounts to little more than an external performance. It doesn't *mean* enough to us. If only we were fully conscious of what we are doing and why we are doing it and what it all means, then surely our worship would have far more effect on us, and overflow more into our daily lives.

And that, dear Reader, is what the "liturgical apostolate" sets out to do for you. Never mind the words—we'll explain those later. It is what's behind them that matters. The liturgical apostolate sets out to *help you in your worship*—to make you fully conscious of what you are doing, and why you are doing it—to make it *mean* a lot to you and be interesting and truly helpful; to turn it from something you have just got to do into something that you will love doing; to lift it up from the status of a mere duty and transform it into a privilege and a joy. And surely that is a proposition worth investigating.

How are things with you now? Be honest with yourself! Take your Mass, for instance. You go every Sunday as all practicing Catholics do. But supposing you didn't have to go? Supposing the Pope issued a new decree which said: "Nobody in future need go to Mass more than once a year unless he wants to." Just think of that! You could lie abed Sunday morning, not go to Mass, and it wouldn't be a sin at all. You would wake up on a Sunday morning and say to yourself, "No work today! I can please myself. I can go to Mass if I like. But I'm not bound to go. I can stay in bed if I like. No sin at all. Not even a venial sin." Well, what would you do? . . . You would? I'm not surprised! So would most people, I think! Yet what a pity that is! For it shows that most people go to Mass chiefly because "they gotta go"—not because they want to go!

There are people who would still get up and go to Mass even if they didn't have to go. They are the people who love it.

Many have come to this love through getting to understand a lot about the Mass. They are people who have acquired what is called a "liturgical outlook" on their worship, who vividly realize what they are doing and why they are doing it, and not only rejoice to go to Mass on Sundays when they've "gotta go" but also are delighted if they find it possible to go on weekdays too.

Now you've "gotta go" as things are, because the Pope has issued no such decree as the one I have imagined. And the betting is that he won't. Hence you face fifty-two Sundays every year when—unless some quite serious reason prevents you—you must force yourself out of your bed and get along to the church and be there for a whole Mass. And if you are one of those who wouldn't go unless he had to (and those are numbered by the million, so you needn't be ashamed to admit being among them), then that means you face fifty-two periods of boredom.

Maybe it's only mild boredom, and out of loyalty to your Faith you are quite willing to endure it. But the fact that you rarely go unless obliged to, shows that you *are* bored. But if, by a bit of reading, you could get a point of view that would turn that boredom (however mild) into interest (even moderate interest), then wouldn't that bit of reading be worthwhile?

Some reading is necessary in order to acquire what is called "the liturgical outlook." You need to regard your worship from the point of view of certain "basic ideas." This booklet is an attempt to lay them before you in an intelligible manner, and to help you to fit them together in your mind. These ideas are not just "catechism stuff"—they go much deeper than that, and are much more interesting. Some of them take a bit of thinking about, but if you will take the trouble, you will find it very much worthwhile.

For when you have acquired some grasp of these main ideas which go to form a "liturgical outlook," you will discover that they make a wonderful difference to your worship. You will find that all sorts of things which meant nothing to you before begin to have a meaning. There will be things that you never noticed before but which now arouse your curiosity, and you'll find considerable pleasure in satisfying that curiosity. There will be other things which you'll find yourself wanting to *do*. You'll begin to see your whole Faith in a new light. It won't be just a list of obligations ... things you've got to do or else; things you've got to believe or else; it will be something for which you will thank God continually, with joy and gladness in your heart. That's what the "liturgical outlook" does for people's faith. That's what it can do for you if you will take the trouble to master these "basic notions."

The first of them is the importance of worship, which I have endeavored to explain above. But I haven't by any means exhausted the notion. I have dealt only with that worship which people should give to God from the fact that they are God's creatures. But there is something else, much more wonderful, that can be added, though there is no room to explain it in this chapter. It is the fact that some of us are no mere ordinary men. Ordinary men can worship God with one manpower. They can put into their worship all the force that is in their human nature—but no more than that. Some of us, however, *can* do more than that. We can exceed the powers of human nature because we have been turned, as it were, into supermen and enabled to worship God with one Godpower!

How does that happen? The answer lies in those familiar words in which the Church ends so many of her prayers— "through Christ our Lord!" Our Lord was not only man, but God. He was indeed a man, just as much as you and I are men. But when He worshiped God His Father, He was not limited to what we might call an "output of one manpower." Being God, He could put into His worship all the power of His Godhead, and thus worship with "one Godpower."

And there are ways in which that worship of His can become our worship. Then it is not merely we who worship, but He who worships in us. We can surpass our own limitations because of the transformation (to be explained later) which

Christ our Lord has worked in us; we worship not merely by our own power, but by His power. Thus it is that we, though merely human, can nevertheless worship God with "one Godpower." That, of course, applies only to those of us who have thus been transformed and given powers which are beyond merely human powers. But you, being a Catholic, are one of these; you can worship God in this superhuman way, and can enjoy doing it if only you know how. That, and a number of connected points, is the "good tidings of great joy" which the liturgical apostolate will endeavor to communicate to you.

Discussion Questions

1. How is worship more important for taking us places than are cars?
2. Define religion in terms of worship and moral behavior. Do we sometimes get the two ideas mixed up?
3. One parishioner often daydreams and looks at everything going on around him at Sunday Mass. What is wrong with this? What simple truths of faith can give us a guide as to how we ought to act in church?
4. Another parishioner would rather busy himself with ushering at Mass than praying along with the priest. How widespread is such lack of *interest in* worship? How can religious education and parish life contribute to a fully adult understanding of worship and real interest in it?
5. There are children who flatter their father with lip service but readily turn about and disobey him. Non-Catholics often complain that their Catholic neighbors do this in not living up to Catholic teaching on social justice and charity. Is this true? In what ways would our worshiping God properly reduce these failures?
6. Why do you think it is so easy for us to fail in giving "due notice" or "behaving accordingly" toward our heavenly Father?
7. Catholics who are morally good but readily miss Sunday Mass are like well-behaved children who ignore their father and fail to give him proper reverence. What means can you suggest for bringing the worship of the liturgy closer to our hearts?
8. Discuss the evidence that people are *bored* at Mass because they don't know what the Mass *means*.
9. Explain the difference between worshiping God with "one manpower" and with "one Godpower."

CHAPTER TWO

THE GOOD TIDINGS

UNLESS WE happen to be converts, most of us learned our religion when we were children. We took it in gradually, absorbing it from our environment of home and school and church. Very early we were taught elementary truths about God, our Lord, our Lady, guardian angels, and some saints; we learned some prayers by heart. We were told that God would be pleased if we did certain things, and that He would not be pleased if we did other things. If we pleased God we were on our way to heaven, and if we offended God we might end up in hell. At school we had formal and more explicit

The picture. The triangle represents God, and the Hebrew letters in the center are the Name of God, Yahweh. The three equal "glories" indicate the three Persons in God. The male and female figures represent mankind, who are shown within the triangle because, through divine grace, they **share** in the very life of God Himself, and have towards Him a filial relationship by which they can cry, "Abba! Father!"

teaching which developed all these foundation-truths in further detail, and showed us the relationship between these truths and our duties and our prayers.

Gradually there was formed in us a certain attitude towards God: we learned to regard God primarily as our Creator, and as the Rewarder of good and evil. We saw our place in the scheme of things—as creatures temporarily in this world for the purpose of making our way to heaven. We learned that Christ, by His death on Calvary, had opened the gates of heaven to us; that He founded an infallible Church to guide us, to tell us what is right and what is wrong, and to provide us with marvelous helps, called sacraments, whereby we are aided to do good and avoid evil. And the Church has an official act of worship—the Mass—in which the fruits of Calvary are applied to our souls.

Through the infallible Church, then, we can know with certainty what to believe (our creed); from the Church we have reliable guidance as to what to do (our code); in the Church we have opportunity for adequate worship (our cult). Creed, code and cult—that is religion. This (with a lot of details filled in) more or less summarizes what we learned when young.

And, of course, it is all perfectly true. But we must ever remember that what we learned when young could be absorbed by us only in an immature way; our minds were so limited in their capacity that nothing deeper could be grasped. We must not imagine that our school-Catholicism is an adequate equipment for life. Just as we grew up in other respects, so we need also to grow up in our religion—to have a mature outlook and grasp of all its implications. The pity of it is that the religious mentality or outlook or attitude (it is difficult to hit on *precisely* the right word) of enormous numbers of Catholics remains the same (fundamentally) as that which was formed in their youth. They remain permanently *immature* in their religion.

To make the point clearer, think of a schoolboy who is beginning to learn chemistry. All he will learn will be that within the mental capacity he *then* has—the mere rudiments of the science. He will learn the main properties of solids, liquids and gases; change of state; mixtures and compounds; preparation of a few elements and compounds, and a bit about acids, bases and salts. That is about all he can manage for a long time. Doubtless he takes a boyish delight in the colors of solutions and precipitates, in the stinks and bangs produced in experiments—and he thinks he is getting along splendidly with his chemistry.

Yet he has no conception of the fascinations that await him later, when he matures. In due course, when intellectually capable of absorbing them, he learns such matters as the atomic theory, the periodic table, electrolytic dissociation, stereoisomerism, atomic structure, isotopes . . . he finds that in chemistry there are delights of the mind which exceed beyond description any delights which he previously derived from the colors and smells of his early experiments. His whole outlook on the science of chemistry has completely outgrown his childlike views. These, of course, do not become false: it remains true that A plus B makes a color and C plus D makes a smell and E plus F makes a bang. But it is now clear to him that chemistry amounts to a great deal more than that sort of thing!

Just so, when we were boys and girls learning our religion we absorbed certain information and formed a certain point of view or outlook on our creed, our code, and our cult. And we thought we were getting a good grip on our religion. So we were—but only as far as our then immature minds could grasp it. And just as the small boy busy with smells and colors and explosions has no idea of the wonders of "adult chemistry," so we, in our youth, could have no idea of the wonders of what we might call "adult Catholicism."

By which I do *not* just mean Catholicism as it is *actually* grasped by millions of people over the age of twenty-one. This, alas, is so often of the same kind as that which they grasped in their youth. While maturing physically (and perhaps even intellectually in many ways) they have failed to mature religiously. What I do mean by "adult Catholicism" is that which involves a grasp of matters corresponding to the atomic theory, periodic table, tautomerism and so on of my chemical analogy.

And what matters are these? Chiefly the meaning of supernatural life, the "Mystical Body" doctrine, the relationship of Christians to Christ and to each other in terms of these; the "corporateness" of justification through Christ, of worship with Christ and of salvation in Christ; Catholic life of Mass, sacraments, liturgical year and so forth as seen from this angle.

All these contain wonders and delights for the mind, heart, soul and even body far surpassing whatever elements of our religion we managed to grasp in our youth. Not that what we learned then becomes in any way false—of course not. It certainly is true and *remains* true that we must keep the commandments, obey the Church, frequent the sacraments, and go to Mass. But from what is called the "liturgical outlook" (which embodies that adult Catholicism I have tried to describe), it becomes clear that Catholicism amounts to infinitely more than this!

Of all the things that have to be explained I am inclined to think that the most fundamental—that which comes logically first—is the idea of supernatural life, or sanctifying grace (to give it its other name). If this is understood, then "Mystical Body" doctrine becomes intelligible. And once that is grasped, all the rest of the "liturgical outlook" can be built up upon it and expressed in terms of it. Hence I shall tackle first of all this subject of "supernatural life."

And the obvious point from which to begin is *natural* life. We are familiar with three forms of it—plant life, animal life, human life. Precisely what life is we do not know; that is a question which biologists have never solved and probably never will solve. But that does not prevent us from knowing a lot *about* life. We know that each form of life is limited in its capabilities. Plants cannot do animal things, and animals cannot do human things.

On a beautiful spring morning a thrush may experience such a feeling of well-being that he opens his beak and expresses himself in exquisite song. The daffodils at the foot of his tree may be equally thriving in their own way—but they cannot sing about it. Yet a man who likewise feels that life is particularly good that morning might very well sing—though *his* song would have words to it because speech is within the power of human nature. Suppose, however, that a thrush which had strayed into Missouri burst forth into a nostalgic ditty about his "Old Kentucky Home," then he would not be acting according to his nature. He would be acting according to human nature, which is *above* his own. Now the Latin word for "above" is *super*. Hence this imaginary thrush would be acting *supernaturally*—doing something supernatural.

Another example. The different forms of life act differently with regard to their food. Plants wait for it to come to them (in the form of soluble salts from the earth). Animals go and get it (whether it be grass in a field or deer in a forest). Man not only procures his food but, when he wants to, he also cooks it. Now if a barren fig-tree started wandering round in search of a nice succulent dung-hill, or if a wolf were discovered rigging up a spit on which to cook a newly killed deer, each would be acting *super*naturally. The tree would be acting according to animal nature; and the wolf according to human nature.

The only possible explanation for such behavior would be that somehow the tree had become endowed with a share in animal nature, and the wolf with a share in human nature. For each would be doing something for which it does not, by its own nature, possess the requisite powers. It must, therefore, be sharing in that type of life which belongs to a nature above *(super)* its own—that is *supernatural life.*

Of course there are not, in fact, any thrushes, fig-trees or wolves capable of these astonishing supernatural actions! We can only imagine them, and are powerless to make these creatures of our imagination exist in reality. But that does not apply to God. He can not only imagine anything imaginable, but, if He wants to, He can create it as a reality. So far as we can make out He has not desired to make any plants or animals share in the type of life higher than their own natural life (unless, perhaps, Balaam's loquacious ass was an instance!)

But He *has* done it in the case of man! For He has invited man to share in divine happiness. And that is not natural to man at all. The happiness natural to man is *human* happiness; divine happiness is what is natural to *God*. To enjoy it is therefore a divine activity, above human nature. If man is to do that, then he has to act *super*naturally; for that he needs supernatural life of the type corresponding to the activity. For a divine activity he would have to have a share in divine life.

And that, best beloved, is precisely what God has given him! Besides his natural life he is given "a created participation in the divine nature" (as theologians call it), and this makes him capable of certain activities which belong properly to God alone and exceed the powers of human nature. In particular, man thereby becomes capable of enjoying God's perfections—that is, of being happy in the way that God is happy (not in a merely human way). This is called the "beatific vision." And because man has no right whatever to this created participation in the divine nature, and has it only through God's goodness or graciousness, it goes also by the name of *grace*.

Beyond doubt many Catholics do not see this point with any vividness. They do not think of grace as sharing in God's own life and powers. Their notions are a bit hazy and inadequate. They regard grace, for instance, as a beautiful garment of the soul which makes it pleasing in God's sight; or else as a kind of ticket of admission into heaven. Which is rather like regarding the health (say) of a young man as the good color in his cheeks or as the doctor's certificate whereby he qualifies for some job.

These notions have, indeed, a measure of truth, but they are too superficial, and grace, when viewed this way, does not seem to be anything very exciting. But if it is thought of and understood as a *life*—as a sharing in that sort of life which belongs by nature to God alone—then it is prized as something unspeakably wonderful, resulting in utterly astounding consequences which entrance the mind and warm the heart.

The first consequence is that when we are given grace we cease to be merely ordinary men and women and become, as it were, supermen. We are lifted above the natural plane on which all other creatures exist, and are brought into the closest intimacy with God Himself. For, without ceasing to be God's creatures, we become also God's sons. We are His sons and daughters in a very real and true sense. Not in the same sense that Christ our Lord is the Son of God—for He is begotten by the Father in the same divine nature as the Father's own. Our sonship is not by nature, but by adoption.

But this means far more than human adoption. If a man adopts a son he may treat the boy in every way *as if* he were his own son; yet the fact remains that the life of the boy was not imparted to him by the man whom he has learned to call "Father." Adoption on the human plane is but a fiction. But adoption by God involves a fact—we become truly God's sons because God does actually impart to us His own type of life (natural and uncreated in Him, supernatural and created in us). And since we *have life* from God we really *are* His sons—not by way of convention, but in fact. When we call God "Our Father" we name Him *truly*.

And a second consequence is that, being sons of God, we are heirs to heaven. We are not, indeed, enjoying God's kind of happiness yet—our bodies have to die before that happens. But we are definitely qualified for or equipped for enjoying that kind of happiness. We have already got those powers which—when we come into the appropriate circumstances—will enable us to see and enjoy God in the beatific vision. Men without the supernatural life of grace are like men born blind and living in a dark cellar. Even supposing they were to be led out into the light they could still see nothing. But we, who have grace, are like people with the power of sight. At present we see nothing, or almost nothing, of God because we are still in the darkness of this earthly life. We only see God by faith "as through a glass, darkly."

But we know that we have the *power* to see Him—we are not blind. We can look forward to being delivered from our dark cellar, passing through the door of death. Then we shall emerge into the light of God's glory and shall be able to "see Him face to face." That is what grace does for us!

Those of us who have this life of grace are enormously privileged. For nobody has any right to it whatever. And not everybody has it—though, but for a fearful tragedy at the very beginning of human history, everybody *might* have had it.

When God first created Adam and Eve He gave to them not only their natural human lives, but also this life of grace we have been discussing here. And besides that He gave sundry lesser privileges—one of which was that though Adam and Eve were mortal (that is, capable of dying) they were in fact going to be spared death. After some time spent in a knowledge of God, imperfect yet sufficient to guide them in living according to God's will, they were to be granted the full and perfect knowledge of God (with its attendant perfect happiness) in the beatific vision. They would come to this without having to die first. So also would all their descendants. That was God's original loving and generous plan.

But unfortunately Adam did not do God's will—he preferred his own will. Instead of pleasing God he chose to please his wife. By thus insulting and disobeying God he committed the first, or "original" sin. Now we must always remember that God is not only infinitely good, but He is infinitely just. It would not have been consistent with His justice to go on giving privileges to rebels! So the privileges were discontinued, and Adam was given his rights—and only his rights.

Nothing really due to him in virtue of his human nature was taken away from him—only the "extras." So he was now no longer exempt from death. Worse still, he now had only his natural human life—which, as we have seen, is not sufficient for enjoying the beatific vision.

The consequences of this were appalling! For Adam could not pass on to his children what he didn't have. His children were *born* as Adam himself had *become*—destined to die and possessing no kind of life except natural life. No *super*natural life. No capacity for enjoying God. No share in the divine nature. No filial relationship with God. The same with the next generation—and the next—and the next—and so on for all time, right down to us and beyond us.

Unless God had done something about it, this meant that all generations of the human race were ruined—rendered incapable of enjoying God in heaven. Even if, by some strange supposition, they could get to heaven they would not know they were there; for they could no more enjoy God than a blind man could enjoy a lovely view. Lacking any share in the divine life, they could not act according to divine nature in enjoying divine happiness.

This is the condition in which all of us came into existence. It is a condition which would never have been were it not for the original sin committed by Adam. That is why it is called the "state of original sin." It is not that we (or any other newborn babes) had actually done anything wrong or offended God in any way. Not at all. But the point is that we had nothing except that to which we were entitled by our status as human beings. Everything which was our due we were given: God did us no wrong in creating us like this. Nevertheless the fact remains that even with the fullest and most perfectly developed of human powers we still could not get to heaven. That can only be done by a privilege—the privilege of sharing in God's kind of life by possessing grace.

How, then, was grace given to us? How was the harm done by Adam's original sin put right? The answer to those questions is the most astonishing and beautiful story in the world. It is the most moving revelation of God's infinite wisdom, of His inexhaustible power and—above all—of his boundless love.

"By this hath the charity of God appeared towards us, because God hath sent His Only-begotten Son into the world, that we may live by Him," says St. John. There came, as a member of the ruined human race, the very Son of God! He was the Son of God the Father, not by adoption, but by nature. Divine life was natural to Him. Yet, when He was made flesh and dwelt amongst us, human life was also natural to Him. And as He shared our human life, He brought it about that we could share His divine life. "I am come," He said, "that they may have life, and have it more abundantly."

The disobedience of Adam under the tree of Paradise was wiped out by the obedience of Christ on the tree of the Cross. All of us entered this world subject to the death sentence, and equipped with merely natural powers, because the life which we had was only natural life derived from Adam. But now we look beyond temporal death to eternal life, which we can enter with supernatural powers provided that we have supernatural life derived from Christ. Our natural life came to us by a process of natural generation from Adam. And the marvelous thing which Christ had done is to arrange that *super*natural life may come to us by a process of *super*natural generation from Himself. He has brought it about that we may be related to Him in the supernatural order in a way which parallels our relationship to Adam in the natural order.

Thus He is the "Second Adam." "Adam," as St. Paul wrote to the Romans, "was the type of Him who was to come.... If one man's fault brought death on a whole multitude, all the more lavish is God's grace, shown to a whole multitude—that free gift He has made us in the grace brought by One Man—Jesus Christ!" Or, as he reminded the Corinthians, "just as all have died with Adam, so with Christ all may be brought to life."

This *life* which Christ won for us, and which He imparts to us, is the very kernel of the Christian message; that He has raised us up above our natural plane unto sonship of God the Father and brotherhood of Himself is the essence of the "Gospel" (which means "good tidings"). An understanding of the why and the how of all this is the key to our creed; a vivid consciousness of it is the motive of our code; and a joyously intelligent reaction to it is the inspiration of our cult. The doctrine of sanctifying grace, in fact, illuminates, informs and enlivens our whole religion and leads us on to comprehend "in all its breath and length and height and depth the love of Christ—to know what passes knowledge!"

How jejune, by contrast, is that view which sees in our religion little more than a collection of "do's and don'ts" coupled with a set of aids for the avoidance of sin and the collection of merits all aimed at the ultimate welfare of the individual. Yet how many there are who seem to get but little further than this in their outlook on their faith!

Discussion Questions

1. Summarize some of your childhood knowledge of creed, code, and cult. How has your grasp of these truths changed and deepened as you have become adults?
2. Do you think we know enough about our faith? What parts do we seem to know best? To know least? What indications of insufficient grasp of these truths by Catholics of your acquaintance can you recall from their conversations about religion, social problems, Mass attendance, the place of the Church in life, etc.?
3. What is there in the way religion is sometimes taught and the sacraments administered that keeps Catholics from applying religious truths to their daily life?
4. How do the three grades of *natural* life help one to understand *supernatural* life?
5. Discuss different ways of thinking of grace, e.g., grace as a ticket to heaven, as divine life, etc. Which is the best way?
6. Compare adoption of an orphan child with our adopted sonship before the Father.
7. How is grace, considered as making us heirs of heaven, like a still unused *power* of vision?
8. Why was it not cruel of God to take away the "extras" of grace from Adam and Eve and their posterity because of original sin?
9. Just how did original sin affect the destiny of Adam and the human race as far as supernatural life is concerned?
10. To what events do the "Good Tidings" refer?
11. Why do we call Christ the "second Adam"?

CHAPTER THREE

SHARING DIVINE LIFE

THE MYSTICAL BODY OF CHRIST

IF THE NOTION of sanctifying grace as the supernatural life of the soul is now clear, we are in a position to understand another idea which is part and parcel of that "mature Catholicism" described in the previous chapter. This is the idea of the "Mystical Body of Christ." We must understand that it is only through the Mystical Body that we acquire our personal share in the divine life; and that it is within the Mystical Body that our personal activities in the supernatural order can come to fruition.

We saw that grace is a share in the divine life; and that we are given it by God. The question we now examine is: *how* does God give us a share in His own kind of life? Does He give it to each of us directly? No! That is not His way. God gives life (of any kind) *directly* only in circumstances which are quite exceptional. For instance, when He created Adam. Adam's life came from no creature but direct from God. The life of all other men, however, comes only indirectly from God, for it originates directly from each one's parents. That is normal among living things: trees get their life from pre-existing trees, horses from pre-existing horses, and men from pre-exist-

The picture. The Mystic Vine, of which the triumphant Christ is the Head, is shown growing along the arms of the Cross, by the power of which we become branches of the Vine, members of the Mystical Body.

ing men (although, in the last-named race, the individual soul is, of course, created by God). Though all life comes ultimately from God, any individual life comes from some being endowed by God with the *power to impart* life.

But that, it would seem, proves nothing about the way in which we get the life of grace. For the examples quoted do not involve any change in the *level* or *plane* of life. The resulting trees, horses or men have a type of life no higher than the trees, horses or men from which their lives were derived. Whereas acquiring the life of grace *involves a change of level*— from the merely human life, upwards, to a share in divine life.

True enough; but we have also in nature instances which are analogous; we have processes whereby there is a conferring of life which *does* involve a change in the level or plane of existence.

To illustrate this I beg to introduce to American readers a famous old Yorkshire song called *"On Ilkley Moor ba t'at!"* It is quite amusing and yet, at the same time, instructive. The words *"ba t'at"* are Yorkshire dialect meaning "without a hat"; and the first verse relates how a young man went courting his girl on the cold and windswept moor near Ilkley, and was seen by his friends hastening to his tryst without any hat. Wherefore, in the second verse, his friends solemnly warn him,

*"Tha wilt catch tha death o' cold
On Ilkley Moor ba t'at!"*

with the result that in the third verse he will be buried and eaten by worms; in the fourth verse ducks eat these worms; in the fifth verse his friends eat these ducks, and reach the conclusion, in the sixth verse,

"Then we shall all 'ave eaten thee!"

The conclusion I want to draw is somewhat different, but is equally clear. There were some bits of matter (after the hatless episode) which had no sort of life whatever. They had "caught their *death* o'cold." But soon they became endowed with animal life (in the worms and then in the ducks) and finally were raised, at the banquet in the penultimate verse, to a share in the human life such as they had had before their original fall! Thus they changed their level or plane of existence—from mineral, to animal, to human. And this successive endowment with a higher form of life came to them each time through a process of becoming part of a pre-existing organism already living with animal or with human life (as the case may be). The conclusion is, then, that it was only by *becoming part of an organism* that they acquired their *new sort* of life.

Now we can see how God goes about giving to us a *new sort* of life. We are to be given a share of divine life. Therefore we are to become *part of an organism already living with divine life*. God does not give grace to each of us directly; instead He has constituted (through the work of Christ our Lord) a grace-filled organism already living with divine life, and has equipped this organism with power to absorb into itself human beings who, by their own nature, have but a lower form of life. This is the organism which we attempt to study in this chapter. Just as something which lives merely by animal life (such as a duck) can be absorbed into a human body and thus be given a share in human life, so also something living merely by human life (such as a man) can be absorbed by this divine organism and thus be given a share in the divine life.

As this last paragraph is a bit complicated, I beg of readers to go over it again two or three times till they are quite satisfied that they have seen the point. For it is *the point* of the whole chapter. In fact it is a cardinal point for the entire understanding of liturgy.

The point, then, is that there exists an organism which, by making us part of itself, endows us with a share in its own life; that this life is above our natural life, is *super*natural life—is, in fact, the same sort of life which God has. This is the way in which we acquire a share in divine life. Not by direct, individual, and personal donation to each of us by God, but by becoming part of this pre-existing and divinely-living organism.

So far I have *stated* the existence of this supernatural organism. But can its existence be *proved?* Most certainly it can—from the words of our Lord and from St. Paul.

Our Lord said to His apostles: "I am the true vine, and it is my Father who tends it . . . the branch that does not live on in the vine can yield no fruit of itself; no more can you, if you do not live on in me. I am the vine, you are its branches! If a man lives on in me, and I in him, then he will yield abundant fruit; separated from me, you have no power to do anything" (John 15:1-6).

He is there stating, in various ways, that the relationship which exists between Himself and His followers is the same as that which exists between a vine and its branches. It is a vital relationship, not merely one of contiguity. Branches are not stuck onto a vine like arms onto a sign-post; the branches *belong*—they are *living*. Moreover, they are living with the *same life* as the vine, deriving that life from the fact that they are part of the organism of the vine. It is the vine's life that is their life. Our Lord's reference to fruit-bearing shows that it is this vital relationship that He means. Just as the life by which the branches live is none other than the life of the vine itself, so—He indicates—the life by which His followers live is none other than His own life. *He and they form one organism.*

St. Paul explains precisely the same point, though in different terms, when he wrote to the Corinthians (1 Cor. 12:12ff.) that "a man's body is all one, though it has a number of different organs; all this multitude of organs goes to make up one body." Together they are, says he equivalently, *one organism.* "And so it is with Christ . . . you are Christ's body, members of it, depending on one another!" That is: you and Christ *form but one organism.* He says the same thing to the Romans (12:4): "Each of us has one body, with many different parts . . . just so we, though many in number, form one body in Christ." St. Paul is very fond of this "body"-simile, and makes frequent use of it to indicate the manner after which we are united to Christ and share with Him one life which is His life.

What sort of life is it that we thus share with Him? Is it His human life? He was a man, and we are men, and so we share one kind of life ... is that it? Certainly not. Because at that rate all human beings, by the mere fact of being human, would be sharing in Christ's life. Moreover that sort of sharing does not involve any organic relationship like that of members to body or branches to vine.

To have such a relationship there must be but one single life-principle, one source of vital energy which is at the same time in Christ and in us—something which we share with Him and which we derive from Him. Our physical lives do not come from Him—they come from our parents. The life we share with Christ is that other sort of life we discussed in the second chapter—the supernatural life called grace. That is divine life. He has it by rights for He is God. We have it only by privilege for we are but human. But seeing that we are part of one organism with our Lord, like branches of a vine or members of a body, then, though only human, we do share His divine life.

About the name of this organism—it is St. Paul's terminology which has been taken into use (though a distinguishing adjective has become attached to it). "You are Christ's body," says St. Paul. But what *is* a body? What is it *for*? It is an organism through which a person can express himself and work upon his environment; an organism which a person needs to use if his actions are to have any effect beyond, or outside of, himself.

For example: I am a human person, possessing human nature, body and soul. I am trying to express myself to you readers at this moment. And I need to use my body to do it. I have to make my fingers actuate the keys of a typewriter in a manner decided by my understanding and reproduced in muscular action by the help of my memory (which are powers of my soul). Your eyes, parts of your living body, will (I trust) abstract meaning from them and store the meanings away in your memory. Thus my person acts on your person: through my soul-actuated body, by means of material things (typewriter, printing press, etc.) to your soul-actuated body, to your person. That is the human way. My body is thus the medium through which I express myself and act upon you; and it consists of the fingers which work these keys, of nerves, muscles, eyes, brain . . . and all these things are living with the one physical life of my soul. All these things together *make up a body for me.*

Now once upon a time the Second Person of the Blessed Trinity desired to work among—to act upon—men. So, by the Incarnation, He took to Himself a human body and soul like ours, and used them to do His work among men. The most important of all His works was the offering of sacrifice on Calvary. As a result of this His body and soul became separated in death. But He joined them together again in the resurrection, and took them to heaven in the ascension. Then that body of His left the earth and was no more active among men.

So if He intended, after the ascension, to do any more work among men, He must either bring that body back again (as He will do when He comes to judge men) or else He must use some other body. And, until the last judgment, He has chosen to do the latter, i.e., to make use of some other body. This time it is not a physical body like the one born of our Lady. It is, instead, that organism we have been discussing above—the one which St. Paul likens to a body. It is the organism which consists of all those human beings who have been raised to a share in that divine life which belongs to Christ.

They are very rightly called a body because, like a human body, they all live as one organism vivified by one soul; and the resulting organism is the instrument of a person in expressing himself. This time the person is divine—the Second Person of the Blessed Trinity. (Incidentally the soul also is divine and is the Third Person of the Blessed Trinity—but that is not the point I am at present trying to make.) But this organism does for Him just what my body does for me. I am living in all these various organs which share my life; I act through them and they make up a body for me. So also Christ is living in all those men who share His life; He acts through them and they make up a body for Him. They are Christ's body.

They are not, of course, a physical body, animated by a human soul. Nor are they merely a moral body united only by a common purpose, such as "the governing body" of a school. It is a sort of body which has no exact parallel in the natural order. So it ought to have some other name, to show it is neither a physical nor a moral body.

For about eight centuries Christian writers could not think of any name suitable for such a unique organism as this one in which Christ now lives and works among men. They just had to call it "the Body of Christ" and leave it to the context to make it clear whether they were talking about this unique body or about the physical body which had gone to heaven. But finally a writer called Ratramnus in the ninth century used the phrase "Mystical Body" to indicate the mysteriousness of this marvelous supernatural organism. And his phrase somehow stuck, and is in general use to this day.

Let us take another look at this organism—the Mystical Body, as I shall henceforth call it. Let us see what it means for us. It means that, quite apart from the Blessed Sacrament (in which our Lord's physical body—and blood and soul and divinity—are present, though not in "usable" form), Christ is still with us. He "descended from heaven" in order to save and sanctify mankind. In Palestine, and by means of His physical body, He taught men and healed their ills; He adored His Father in prayer, and gave Him supreme glory in the sacrifice of Calvary. And now He continues those same activities, but He uses His Mystical Body instead. Hence He is no longer limited to Palestine and to the years 4 B.C. till 30 A.D. (or whatever the correct dates may have been). He teaches and sanctifies men and prays and sacrifices to His Father throughout all places and all time.

His Mystical Body (another name for which is the Catholic Church) is thus, in a certain manner, a prolongation of the

Incarnation. The Church *is* Christ still living and working amongst us. "Christ is the Head," says St. Paul, "to which the whole Church is joined, so that the Church is His Body" (Eph. 1:22). The Church, of course, is also an organization of pope and bishops and clergy and laity. But we must see in it much more than that. The Church has a unity deeper than that of a school consisting of teachers and taught; or of an army consisting of commanders and commanded. Though the Church is indeed an organization, the even more important truth is that it is an *organism;* it is that organism which lives with the one life of Christ; it is a body; it is the Mystical Body of Christ!

The late Holy Father, Pope Pius XII, wrote a very beautiful encyclical about all this. Every reader of this chapter, if he really "means business" and truly intends to learn what he ought to learn, should get a copy of this encyclical and study it most carefully. Here I propose merely to quote and to comment on a few sentences of outstanding importance.[1]

"The name 'Body of Christ' means more than that Christ is the Head of the Mystical Body; it means also that He, after a certain manner, so lives in the Church that she may be said to be another Christ" (n. 66).

"It is Christ who baptizes through the Church, He who teaches, governs, absolves, binds, offers, and makes sacrifice" (67).

"Our union with Christ in the Body of the Church . . . is very close indeed; it is so intimate that a very ancient and constant tradition of the Fathers . . . teaches that the divine Redeemer, together with His social Body, constitutes one mystical person, or—as St. Augustine expresses it—'the whole Christ' " (n. 82).

"Christ, the mystical Head, and the Church, together constitute one new man, joining heaven and earth in the continuance of the saving work of the Cross. Christ, Head and Body, is the whole Christ" (n. 93).

[1] Numbers refer to paragraphs in the edition (prepared for study club use) published by the America Press, 70 East 45th St., New York.

"No greater glory, no higher dignity, no honor more sublime can be conceived than that of belonging to the Holy, Catholic, Apostolic and Roman Church, wherein we become members of this one venerable Body, are governed by one august Head, filled with the one divine Spirit, nourished during this earthly exile with one doctrine and one Bread of angels, until at last we come to enjoy in heaven one everlasting happiness" (n. 107).

From all this we can see that the acts of the Church in glorifying God and sanctifying men are the acts of Christ—of the "whole Christ" of whom we are privileged to be members. It follows that in these acts He sacrifices, praises God and sanctifies men through us—for He uses us as instruments. Hence when we worship God in our social capacity as members of the Mystical Body we are doing something which far surpasses our individual powers; for the worship we thus offer is the worship of Christ, the God-man, our Head of whom we are members. Any worship we can offer to God of ourselves is inadequate. But by reason of our incorporation into Christ we can "through Him and with Him and in Him" give to God the Father "all honor and glory" (as the priest says in Mass).

This belonging in the Body of Christ (or "incorporation," as it is called) is the very basis of what we call "liturgy." The word itself we shall have occasion to discuss later. What I want to emphasize here is the fact that it is only because of "incorporation" that there is any such thing as "liturgy." And it is precisely because we *are* all so incorporated that liturgy does concern all of us (and not just the clergy). The "liturgical movement" and all that it stands for is but a development in action of this basic doctrine of the "Mystical Body of Christ."

Understand that, and you have the key to everything in the realm of liturgy. Be ignorant of that, and all that is liturgy will seem to you just a sort of persnickety puttering with various esthetic fads for which sensible practical people just haven't got the time!

And so, dear reader, I beseech you to spare no time and trouble to get a vivid grasp of this wonderful doctrine. It is the basis, not only of liturgy, but even of Christianity. Master it, understand it, make it a part of your mental outlook, and you will be astonished how it will transform and ennoble and lift up and vivify and gladden your whole faith. "Let us thank God, through His Son, in the Holy Spirit," wrote St. Leo in a sermon quoted in the Christmas Office, "for He has made us alive with Christ, that we might be in Him as new creatures! . . . Be conscious, O Christian, of your dignity! You are now made a sharer in the divine nature, so do not degenerate to merely natural standards. Remember of whose Body you are a member!"

Finally, I want to add a caution. The Holy Father reminds us in his encyclical that in studying this doctrine "we are dealing with a hidden mystery which, during our exile on earth, can never be completely unveiled, never altogether understood, nor adequately expressed in human language" (n. 95). Now he himself, in the course of some fifteen thousand words, had space in which he could express detailed qualifications of all sorts of statements which I, in a short chapter, can give in the barest outline only. Hence, if there be any doubt of the precise sense in which I mean any particular statement to be understood, it should be compared with the encyclical. A general principle against misunderstanding is that "any explanation of this mystical union is to be rejected if it makes the faithful in any way pass beyond the order of created things, and so trespass on the divine sphere that even one single attribute of the eternal God could be predicated of them in the proper sense" (n. 94).

I draw attention to this for I am well aware that highly trained theologians would be able to pick holes in what I have written, saying that this or that statement, as I have put it, does not exclude interpretation in some manner savoring of Apollinarianism, Docetism, Sabellianism or other hoary old heresies. Maybe they're right. But if I have to add to my statements qualifying phrases designed to exclude all possibility of misinterpretation, then the whole chapter would become hopelessly unintelligible, and as heavy and unattractive as the average textbook of theology. And I'm not writing a textbook of theology—I'm attempting a "popular explanation" of a truth so deep that not even a theological pundit can explain it fully.

It is from this standpoint that the chapter should be judged. It will have achieved all that I can hope for if readers have persevered, in spite of the intrinsic difficulty of the subject, in reading thus far; and if the phrase "Mystical Body of Christ" has ceased to be to them mere words, and has begun really to *mean something*—even if some of the notions be not so meticulously accurate as to satisfy professional theologians. And, while I am about it, I may as well add that this holds, also, for all the remaining chapters of this book.

Discussion Questions

1. Why is it reasonable that God should give us a new sort of life by making us part of an organism already living with divine life?
2. Refer to as many New Testament passages as you can on our sharing in grace through living membership in the Church.
3. What makes the organism of the Mystical Body live?
4. Point out instances in the news of the past week (or in your personal experience) which illustrate either the living out or the neglect of the Mystical Body idea.
5. Compare our contact with others through our human bodies with our contact with God through the Mystical Body.
6. Describe Christ's work and position as head of the Mystical Body.
7. Explain how the Mystical Body differs from Christ's physical body and from what we call moral bodies.
8. How is the Church an extension of the Incarnation into every generation?
9. Explain how worship for you as a member of the Church differs from natural pagan worship.

CHAPTER FOUR

OF THINGS VISIBLE AND INVISIBLE
THE SACRAMENTAL PRINCIPLE

OF MY VISIT to the United States in 1949-50 I have many happy memories. One of the most exciting—and one which often comes back to my mind—was a night-ride in the driving-cab of a huge Diesel locomotive. This was arranged for me by the pastor of one of the places where I had been preaching. I had to leave his parish late one Saturday night in order to get to the next place where I was due to start on Sunday morning; and as one of his parishioners was a rather important official of a certain railroad, he managed to get for me the privilege of making my journey in the driving-cab.

The picture. Christ likened His followers to the birds of the air; hence birds were used in the catacombs from the earliest days as symbols of the faithful. The fountain represents the Church, which is a reservoir of grace, replenished by the stream gushing forth from the pierced side of Christ (the Chi-Rho sign). Chi and Rho are the first two letters in the Greek name of Christ, and, when superimposed upon one another, are a traditional symbol of Christ Himself. The seven panels of the fountain remind us of the Church's seven Sacraments.

We left at 10:30 p.m. and for about five hours I sat with the engineer and the fireman behind the great headlight of the Diesel while we pounded along through the night. I was received in most friendly fashion and treated as an honored guest in the driving-cab. The engineer explained to me everything I asked about—the dials and gauges inside, the lights and signals outside.

And, while admiring the wonderful skill wherewith the engineer exerted perfect control at all times over the gigantic power-unit in which we sat, and the thundering mass of train behind us, I reflected much upon the tremendous importance of *signs*. Almost everything seemed to be connected with or depend upon some *sign*. It was a sign which told the engineer to start the train on its journey. He drove at eighty miles an hour when certain signs by the track told him it was safe to do so; he reduced speed to fifty or to forty miles an hour when other signs indicated that some curve ahead required this; he went ahead confidently when some green light told him the next section was clear; he brought the train to a standstill when some red light told him he must stop.

His very control of the train was dependent on *signs*—for he knew exactly how fast he was going, what was the air-pressure in his braking system, what was the temperature of his lubricating system, what was the amperage in his lighting system . . . he knew all about everything to do with his engine. He knew it all from the readings of the various dials in front of him. They were there for the precise purpose of signifying all these things which he needed to know. How important are *signs!*

But also another thought struck me: how powerless, in themselves, are signs. They do not *cause* the things which they signify. It was not the greenness of the light ahead which removed all obstacles from the next section of the track. It was not the finger pointing to 80 on the dial which made the train go at eighty miles an hour. And so with all the other indicators and dials and signals. All of them just told something to the engineer, but not one of them produced whatever it was that they told him.

That is the way of things with merely human signs. But there are just a few signs which have been arranged by God, not by men. And God's signs are very far from being powerless. God's signs have God's power behind them. They signify, indeed—as do human signs; but they do much more than that—they also *effect* what they signify. God has given them the power to effect in the supernatural order what they signify in the natural order.

Let us put it another way. We are not just souls—that is, merely spiritual beings. Nor are we just bodies—merely material beings. We are in fact composite beings—*embodied souls*. And, as I attempted to explain in Chapter III, our bodies are the instruments of our souls. If I want to do something to your soul—for instance, make your understanding consider some truth—then I have to do something to your body. Either I must make meaningful sounds reach your ears, as in preaching; or else I must make meaningful sights like this printed page be displayed before your eyes, as in writing. I can only get at your soul *through your body*.

Now God desires to produce certain effects in your soul; because He can do all things He does not *need* to use your body to "get at you." Just occasionally He does do something to somebody's soul without affecting his body at all. But this is not normal. Usually He does what He wishes by means of certain arrangements which He employs as His ordinary ways of dealing with souls, and in these He *does* use your body because doing it like that suits human nature better. There are things you can see or hear or touch—material things—which, by God's power, can produce effects in your soul. The effects, moreover, are not merely natural, but are supernatural—in the sense explained in Chapter II.

We call this the *"sacramental principle."* It means that God has attached power to certain *natural* signs whereby they produce *supernatural* effects. For example: there is a natural sign of cleansing which, by the power of God, is the cause of supernatural cleanness. There is a natural sign of feeding which, by the power of God, causes supernatural nourishment, etc.

It was Christ our Lord who first made this arrangement. How He did it is a mystery to us: we cannot understand it fully. But this "sacramental principle" is at the very basis of our dealings with God and God's dealings with us. Hence we ought to study it and take the trouble to understand as much of it as may be within our capacity. For there are at least certain facts that we can grasp, even though we cannot comprehend quite how God causes them to be.

One fact is that by means of this sacramental principle God can make things exist in a manner totally outside our experience or imagination. Because in the sacraments (those particular signs to which Christ attached effectiveness) the things which are signified actually happen, as I have stated. But there is nothing else in the whole of creation which has a real existence in signs. There are many signs—but they only signify and do not cause. These signs, however, not only signify—they also cause. It is therefore only in *these* signs that there is an underlying reality.

Now we seem to have run into a very tough bit of thinking. But there is no way around it. I warned you earlier that in this book you would not be getting mere "catechism stuff." I could, of course, let you off this bit of mental effort, but I can't see that it would do any good to leave you without any understanding of this sacramental principle. Easier to cut it out, certainly. But that would only leave you unequipped for any better understanding of the Mass and of the sacraments than that which you probably have now. So please bear with me a bit longer and let us see if we cannot get some clear notions of this "sacramental order of existence."

Think of our Lord's death on the cross. Did it really happen? Of course it did: we all know that. It was a historical fact. It was a *real* death. Yet, at this moment, His death is in your mind because you are thinking about it. Now is that death which is in your mind, a real death of our Lord? No!—as it exists in your mind it is only imaginary. So now you have examples of two ways in which the death of Christ can take place: in the order of history (which is a real way), and in the order of ideas (which is an imaginary way).

Now what I am trying to tell you is that since our Lord arranged that it be so, there is a third way in which His death takes place—in the "sacramental order." And (mark this well) this sacramental order is a *real way* and not an imaginary way. It is *just as real as the order of history*. But the qualities of things in the sacramental order are utterly different from the qualities of those same things in the historical order or in the order of ideas.

Sacraments, then, are not like anything else in existence. There were no such things until Christ came to redeem us. But when He came, He created this new order of existence—the sacraments—for the purpose of using them as channels for communicating to us the fruits of His redemption. They are all part of His plan, that part which was not due to be put into effect till our Lord came and which, as St. Paul expressed it to the Ephesians, was till then "a mystery kept hidden from the beginning of time in the all-creating mind of God" (Eph. 3:9).

Two points should be noted about the signifying power of the sacraments: one is that it may be multiple, and the other is that it is in no way constrained by dimensions of time or space. The first means that one and the same sign may signify (and effect in the sacramental order) various realities. For example, baptism signifies cleansing, *but also* dying and rising with Christ.

The second point has been best expressed by St. Thomas Aquinas: "A sacrament is something ordained to signify our sanctification; and three aspects may be discerned in it, namely, the *cause* of our sanctification, which is the passion of Christ; the *essence* of our sanctification, which consists in grace and virtues; and the *ultimate goal* of our sanctification, which is eternal life. All these are signified by a sacrament. Hence a sacrament is not only a commemorative sign of something which is now past, namely, the passion of Christ; it is also a demonstrative sign of something now present and caused in us by the passion of Christ, namely, grace; further it is a prognostic or prophetic sign of something as yet in the future, namely, glory" (*Summa Theologica* III, q. 60, a. 3).

This teaching of St. Thomas is admirably expressed in the beautiful prayer which he himself composed in honor of the greatest of the sacraments, the holy Eucharist: "O sacred Banquet wherein Christ is received: (1) the memory of His passion is renewed, (2) the mind is filled with grace, and (3) a pledge of future glory is given to us!"

Though it is more clear in the holy Eucharist than in any other, the fact is that every sacrament has this triple aspect: it is a *sign* (something perceived by our senses) of invisible realities (imperceptible by our senses) which it causes to exist in this mysterious "sacramental order." And these realities, in their other (or temporal) mode of existence are of the past (the action whereby Christ then redeemed us), and of the present (the action whereby Christ now sanctifies us), and also of the future (the action whereby Christ will glorify us). The whole sacrament is therefore an action of Christ. And yet also, because it is something that involves the use of our bodily senses, it is an action done by us.

What wonderful things are the sacraments! How fully they deserve the title of "the Mysteries of Christ." It is in and through the sacraments that He comes to us—they embody His redemptive actions. And yet, precisely because the sacraments are *our actions also* it follows that the redemptive actions of Christ are our actions. He has "made them over to us," for they are all there in the sacraments. "What was visible in the life of Christ has passed over into the sacraments," said St. Leo the Great (Sermon 74, 2). When it was visible, it was a historic reality. Now that it is signified, it is a sacramental reality. But all Christ's work of salvation and sanctification *is no less real now* as a *signified* reality of the sacramental order, than it once was as a *visible* reality of the historic order.

There are, of course, differences. The obvious difference is that then His redemptive work was visible, whereas now it is not visible but signified. Another difference, of vast importance to us, is the fact that He was then acting alone, through the instrumentality of His physical body; and we had no share in His actions. But now He is acting through the instrumentality of His Mystical Body; and we do share in His action because it is sacramental, and it is we who "do" these sacraments. As the Pope points out in the encyclical *Mediator Dei:*

"Although Christ, universally speaking, has reconciled the whole human race to the Father by His death, yet He has willed that men should come and be brought to His cross by means of the sacraments and the Mass, and so take possession of the fruits which through the cross He has won for them. By this active and personal co-operation the members become ever more and more like their Head, and at the same time the salvation that flows from the Head is imparted to the members themselves; so that each of us can repeat the words of St. Paul, 'With Christ I hang upon the cross; and yet I am alive; or rather, not I; it is Christ that lives in me'" (n. 78: NCWC edition).

In becoming thus participators sacramentally in the very redemptive works of Christ we are, of course, sanctified. And this redounds to God's glory. Not only does God come to us through the sacraments, but through them we go to God. The sacraments are the most important way in which, during this life, we have dealings with God. It is chiefly through these sacramental signs that we adore Him. As we shall see later on, our greatest act of adoration is the Mass.

This statement is literally true *only because* the Mass is a *sacramental* action. If it were not a sacramental action, then either it would not be perfect worship (because it would be merely our act and not Christ's); or else it would not be our act (though it would then be perfect worship because an act of Christ). But because it is sacramental it *is* our act of worship; and because it is sacramental it is *also* Christ's act of worship, and hence perfect. Wherefore we can do an act of worship which is perfect worship. We do it "through Him and with Him and in Him." We must never think of the Mass as something separate from the sacraments, for it is, in fact, the greatest of them all. The Mass is the Eucharist *offered;* and holy Communion is the Eucharist *received*. Both are the same sacrament under different aspects.

That the Mass draws its power from Calvary is a thing that everybody knows. But we must realize also that all the other sacraments too draw their power from the same source. The whole lot of them are the making present, in the sacramental order of existence, of the redemptive work of Christ; and they make that work our work because we are agents in the production or reception of these wonderful signs which He instituted for the very purpose of making His redemptive acts our own.

In these first four chapters we have considered a number of basic notions: those of worship, of sanctifying grace, of the Mystical Body of Christ, and of the sacramental principle. Already it should be clear that these are very closely connected. There is just one other basic notion which I can now explain in terms of what has gone before, and that is what is involved in the term "liturgy."

Originally this word comes from the Greek *leiton,* meaning "people"; and *ergon,* meaning "work." If a Greek citizen did some kind of work which was for the benefit of the people, he was said to have performed a *leiturgia* or "liturgy"; and he himself was termed a *leiturgos* or "liturgist." For instance, if he built a theatre and engaged a troop of actors in order that the general public might enjoy the drama, that was a liturgy. If he built a warship and gave it to the state, that was a liturgy. It was a work which he had done, at his own expense, for the good of the people. But you will notice that it was also something which required the collaboration of the people. Of what use would it be to build a theatre if nobody went to the play? Of what use would a warship be if the citizens did not collaborate by manning it and taking it to sea?

You will note also that the word did not originally have anything to do with religion. If it had kept its general sense until now, we might be referring to such men as Rockefeller and Carnegie as "liturgists"; the institutes, libraries, research centers or hospitals which they set up would be called their "liturgies." For these things were not for themselves; they were for the good of the people; and they are works such that they need the collaboration of the people who would study in them or do research or get cured in them, as the case may be.

Among the various liturgies there were, however, some which were religious. For example, a man might build a temple in honor of one of the pagan gods, and maintain priests and provide sacrifices for the honor of that god. This was regarded as being a benefit for the people for whom the favor of that god would be obtained and who would thus have facilities for the worship of that god. If a man became a priest and devoted his life to such things as the offering of sacrifice—the supreme act of religion—then that was regarded as a liturgy, and he was called a liturgist.

In the course of time the words "liturgy" and "liturgist" became gradually restricted in their meaning and were applied *only* in the sphere of religion. But they still meant religious acts which had the distinguishing qualities of "liturgy" in the original sense: namely, they were works done by some individual man, for the good of the people, and needing the collaboration of the people.

Now think of the work which our Blessed Lord came to do on earth. He undertook the task of redeeming mankind by His sacrifice of the cross. This was preeminently a liturgy. For He was the great High Priest of the redeeming sacrifice; He offered it, not for Himself, but for the good of the people—of the whole of mankind. And it is a work such that it needs the collaboration of the people for, as the Pope says in *Mediator*

Dei, "It is necessary for each member of the human race to get vitally in touch with the sacrifice of the cross, so that the merits which flow from it may be bestowed upon him. . . . If individual sinners are to be purified in the blood of the Lamb, Christians themselves must cooperate" (n. 77).

What Christ did has, therefore, all the characteristics of a "liturgy." It is, in fact, the supreme liturgy, and He is the supreme liturgist. St. Paul expressly refers to Him as "Liturgist" in several places (for instance, in the Epistle to the Hebrews 8:2, where the Greek word used is *leiturgos*). *But* this perfect liturgy of His was not all over and done with when they took Him down from the cross. He is "of the order of Melchisedech" and has an eternal priesthood. He continues His liturgy of giving perfect worship to God the Father and of saving and sanctifying mankind.

But He does it now, not in His physical body in which He lived for a time in this world. Instead He does it sacramentally, through His Mystical Body, the Church. Thus Christ, living on in His Church, continues to offer sacrifice—and that is the Mass. He continues to pray, to praise God and intercede for men. This is the divine office. He continues to sanctify men, giving grace to their souls, healing their spiritual ills, nourishing the supernatural life which He won for them. Hence the sacraments. All these are Christ's liturgy—the work done by Him, on behalf of many, and needing the collaboration of the many.

This liturgy, ever carried on by Christ in His Mystical Body, has now a ritual form because it is carried on by and through the members of His Mystical Body—ourselves. Thus in holy Mass and the sacraments and the divine office there is an official form of words used and actions performed; in fact, a text.

The word "liturgy" has thus a twofold sense. The primary meaning is that work of redemption which Christ our Lord originally carried out in the order of history, and which He now continues in the order of Mystery (the sacramental order) in the form of the Mass, sacraments and divine office. These actions of His are also our actions now because we, as members of His Mystical Body, actually do them. The secondary and derived meaning of the word "liturgy" is that official collection of prayers, readings, hymns, and actions by which Christ's liturgy is continued; in fact, the text of the Mass, sacraments and office. In the chapters which follow, the word "liturgy" will sometimes be used in one sense, and sometimes in the other. But usually it will be clear from the context which sense is intended.

I will end now with the definition given to us by the Pope in *Mediator Dei:* "The sacred liturgy is the public worship which our Redeemer, the Head of the Church, renders to the heavenly Father, and which the society of Christ's faithful renders to its founder and, through Him, to the eternal Father. To put it briefly, it is the integral public worship of the Mystical Body of Christ, Head and members" (n. 20).

Discussion Questions

1. Formulate a brief definition of the "sacramental principal" and explain it in your own words.
2. Why should we consider the visible signs of the sacraments as *normal* ways for God to work supernatural changes in our lives?
3. That Jesus' death on Calvary was a real event of the historical order is clear. Does He really "die" again in the sacramental order? How does this death differ from death as it exists in our thoughts?
4. Why is the sacrament of the Eucharist a commemorative, demonstrative, and prophetic sign all in one?
5. The sacraments make us share in Christ's redemptive action. Explain how our membership in the Mystical Body makes this possible.
6. A parishioner who had to work Saturday nights regularly fasted to be able to receive Communion at Sunday Mass. Why does St. Paul's claim apply to him: "With Christ I hang upon the cross; and yet I am alive; or rather, not I; it is Christ that lives in me"?
7. A volunteer nurse goes about in the community with medicine during an epidemic. Explain how she is carrying out a "liturgy." How can the nurse make her liturgy a part of divine liturgy, i.e., of the redeeming work of Christ?

8. What was the origin of the term *liturgy?*
9. Why must we recognize Christ as the supreme liturgist?
10. Discuss the various ways in which Christ now performs His liturgy *sacramentally* in the life of the Church.
11. What is the difference between "ritual" and "liturgy"? Explain how ritual forms (i.e., the official collections of prayers and actions) derive their value from Christ's liturgy.

CHAPTER FIVE

THE MAKING OF A CHRISTIAN

THE SACRAMENTS, as we saw in the previous chapter, are a marvelous new creation on the part of Christ our Lord. They are like nothing else upon the face of the earth. By their means, those actions whereby Christ redeemed and sanctified mankind are caused to exist in a new and mysterious way in certain signs which He selected for the purpose. And because these signs—the vehicles now of His action—are things which *we* do, it follows that actions of Christ become *our* actions. It is only through the sacraments that we can make His actions ours.

Now the most important of His actions were His death and resurrection. By means of a sign, done by us, but representing (effectively, as is the way with sacraments) His death and resurrection, He makes those actions our actions. Which means that we die with Him and rise with Him to a new life. The sign which He chose for this is what we call baptism. A rite of baptism was in use before He came; we find St. John the

The picture. If the words, "Jesus Christ, Son of God, Saviour," are written in Greek, then the initial letters of each word, when put together, form the Greek word ICTHUS, which means "fish." That is why the fish is a traditional symbol for Christ. And because Christians must be "other Christs" they were often represented in catacomb pictures as little fish. We are brought to the fulness of Christian life in three stages: first we "Little Fish" are immersed in the waters (of baptism), and then we are led by the Holy Ghost (the Dove, in confirmation) to the "Big Fish" (Christ) carrying the basket of bread (the Eucharist).

Baptist using it because it represented a washing—so that those who underwent it manifested their desire to be purified from sin. But, as I said before, the sacraments have sometimes a multiple power of signifying—and this is a case in point. Going down into the water (the way it was done in our Lord's day and for many centuries afterwards in warm climates) represents also going down into a grave—a *dying*. And rising up out of the water represents rising from the grave—a *coming to life*.

And our Lord made this into a sacrament, one of those signs which effect supernaturally what they signify naturally. So, when someone is baptized, he goes through rites which naturally represent burial and resurrection, and also naturally represent cleansing. Wherefore the effects upon his soul are that he dies and rises again in the supernatural order, and is likewise supernaturally cleansed.

This is what St. Paul told the Romans very clearly: "Know ye not, that as many of us as were baptized in Christ Jesus are baptized in his death? For we are buried together with him by baptism into death; that, as Christ is risen from the dead by the glory of the Father, so we also may walk in newness of life. For if we have been planted together in the likeness of his death, we shall be also in the likeness of his resurrection" (Rom. 6:4). You will notice that the Apostle does not say "we were baptized in his death"; he says "in the *likeness* of his death,"—that is, in its representation or sign, which baptism is.

St. Cyril of Jerusalem has a most instructive passage about this in one of his catechetical sermons:

"O extraordinary and paradoxical fact! We do not actually die, are not actually buried and brought to life after crucifixion, but all this happens to us in a likeness; yet our healing is actual. It was Christ who was truly crucified and buried and rose again; but He has given all this to us, so that we, by partaking in the likeness of His passion, might in reality receive its effects. What love beyond measure! Christ suffered the nails in His sacred hands and feet, and yet He gives to me, without suffering and pain, His salvation! So let no one think that baptism is merely the wiping out of sin. . . . We know much more precisely that though it is indeed a cleansing from sin, it is also a sharing in the death and resurrection of Christ. . . . Everything actually happened to Christ. But in your case it is a likeness of His passion and death which happens. His salvation, however, you receive not in mere likeness, but in fact" (Second Mystagogical Catechesis, 5).

When Christ rose from death He "walked in newness of life." He was *different*—He had new powers. So, when we have done that which signifies His death and resurrection (namely, undergone baptism), we also "walk in newness of life" in the supernatural order. Which means, firstly, that we are living with the "Christ-life" of grace, as described in an earlier chapter. And it means, secondly, that we too, have new powers. In this we are likened to Christ, or "conformed to Him" (as St. Paul puts it). There is a name for this "likeness to Christ"—it is called "the baptismal character." The soul of the baptized person is different from that of the unbaptized; it is different because it has power *to do* things which other souls cannot do.

One thing which non-Christian souls are incapable of doing is to give fitting worship to God. They are but natural souls, having only natural life, and so are not really worthy to enter into that close familiarity with God which worship involves. The Christian soul, by contrast, has the life of grace and the dignity of adopted sonship of God. Divine worship is henceforth one of its functions. It is, as St. Thomas Aquinas expresses it, "deputed to worship." And as worship is done through the "Mysteries of Christ"—the sacraments (especially through that sacrament which is also a sacrifice)—this means that in baptism the soul is destined to, or orientated towards the Christian Mysteries.

We reach just the same conclusions (but perhaps come to an even fuller understanding of all that they mean) if we regard baptism from another, equally true, angle. It is the beginning of a new life; and we may describe the beginning of life as "birth." That is how our Lord Himself described it when He was explaining to Nicodemus that merely natural life was an insufficient equipment for the happiness of heaven. "A man cannot see the kingdom of God without being born anew," He said. "No man can enter the kingdom of God unless birth comes to him from water and from the Holy Spirit. What is born by natural birth is a thing of nature; what is born by spiritual birth is a thing of the spirit" (John 3:5, 6).

In baptism, then, by "water and the Holy Spirit" we acquire new life; we are "born again." God imparts to us a life which is of the same kind as His own life—supernatural life, which we studied in Chapter II. And, in the chapter which followed, we saw that when God confers on any living being a type of life above its own—which changes its plane or level of existence—He does not do this directly or individually. He does it by making that being a part of a pre-existing organism which already lives with the higher type of life. This, then, is what happens in baptism. We, who are therein given a share in the divine life, receive it by becoming part of a pre-existing organism already living with the divine life. And we have seen what that organism is: it is the Mystical Body of Christ.

So baptism is a sacrament of *incorporation*. It makes us members of the Mystical Body of Christ. When Christ acts through His Mystical Body He acts through us. His action is our action. That is why the "Mysteries of Christ" are our actions, as well as His actions. But these "Mysteries of Christ" are the worship of God. It is thus through our incorporation into the Mystical Body (that is, through baptism) that we are enabled, given power, to worship. We are "deputed to worship"; we are "conformed to Christ" in His worship. And this conformation is called the baptismal character.

The same result, you see, though reached by a different line of reasoning from a different starting-point.

Let us now repeat—though without any arguments—just what baptism signifies and does. It signifies the death and resurrection of Christ. Hence, it effects, in the supernatural order, that Christ's death and resurrection (now sacramental realities) become *our* death and resurrection. Moreover baptism signifies cleansing. Hence it effects, in the supernatural order, a cleansing of our souls from sin. By rising with Christ we begin a new sort of life—are "born again." Our new life is not a direct, individual gift, but comes from Christ's Mystical Body through which He is acting in this, as in all sacraments. We are thus incorporated into—made members of—that Mystical Body.

Wherefore we have the power to share in the acts of that Body—in particular in the act of worship. We are "deputed to worship"—empowered to do it because now conformed to Christ, having that character which distinguishes the Christian soul from the non-Christian, merely natural, soul.

If that is all clear, we can now go a stage further. Our conformation to Christ is not complete with baptism. The Christian has, indeed, supernatural life as the result of his new birth. But that is not enough—there is more to come. Even in the natural order it is not sufficient merely to have life, as we can see from thinking a while about any new-born babe. It has life indeed; but its powers are so very limited. It is, as a baby, of no use to human society because it can only receive from, and not give to, the rest of mankind. In the course of years there are developed the powers of maturity which render the living human being capable of taking its full part in social life.

So also the Christian soul, new-born in baptism, has powers so limited that it cannot function fully as a useful member of Christian society—the Mystical Body of Christ. It needs further powers which will enable it to give as well as to receive from that Body. It needs yet further conformation to Christ who has, and who exercises, the fulness of spiritual powers as Head of the Body. And so there is a sacrament for effecting this—and it is called *confirmation*. Its external sign is the anointing with oil and laying on of the hands.

Anointings were much used in olden days; there were ointments employed in healing bodily ills, and oils were used in the massage of athletes to develop their strength. Health and strength, then, are signified by this sacramental anointing; in consequence, spiritual health and strength are caused in the supernatural life of the soul.

The laying on of hands was also customary in the conferring of some office or responsibility on a person faced with new duties, or entering a new state of life. In confirmation, then, the Christian is charged with the duties of full participation in the life of the Christian community of the Mystical Body—which involves, in particular, the Christian Mysteries of worship (cf. St. Thomas. *Summa Theol.* III, p. 72, 2).

This explains why confirmation was given immediately after baptism in early days when those to be made Christians were mostly adults. It explains also why confirmation is recognized as a completion of the effects of baptism, conforming the soul still more perfectly to Christ by imparting further powers. The fact that it does this means that it, like baptism (and holy orders, as we shall later see), confers a "character" or likeness to Christ. The characters of all these three sacraments are, according to St. Thomas, progressive sharings in the priestly powers of Christ (*Summa Theol.* III, 63, 3). In confirmation those concerned are the powers to be exercised in the public or social worship of the Church, as contrasted with individual acts of worship.

Hence there is obviously something else to follow in order that the Christian soul, endowed with Christian life and equipped with Christ-like powers, may attain that fulness of union with Christ for which all that has gone before is but a preparation. That sharing in the death and resurrection of Christ which is baptism demands, as its completion, that other sharing in the death and resurrection of Christ which is the Mass. That likeness to Christ conferred in the characters of baptism and confirmation, and which is a sharing in the priesthood of Christ, demands its expression in the exercise of the priesthood through the offering of Christian Sacrifice. Baptism and confirmation thus lead to the Mass: to the Mass, moreover, fully appropriated by the most important act of lay-participation, which is holy Communion.

The Eucharist, then, completes the process of Christian initiation; it is only through baptism, confirmation *and the Eucharist* that a man comes to the complete activation of that Christian life which is his as a member of the Mystical Body. This accounts for the practice of the early Church—which was continued for many centuries—of conferring these three sacraments successively in the one rite of initiation.

How vividly all this was brought home to the Christians of early times, in the magnificent ceremonies of Eastertide, when these were done with their full and glorious ritual, instead of (as now) in a truncated form, shorn of much of their instructive power. Early Christians celebrated at Easter not merely the resurrection of Christ, but also the resurrection of mankind, from the death of sin to the new life of grace. It was the great feast of Christian initiation.

With all sorts of instructions, ceremonies, exorcisms, scrutinies lasting throughout the time we now call Lent, the Christian community prepared those who had but natural life for that incorporation into Christ which would bring them supernatural life. On Holy Saturday evening they all met together; with prayer and song they blessed new fire and lit up their church, replacing darkness with light culminating in the paschal candle which stood for Him who was the "Light that shineth in the darkness."

Then followed the blessing of the font. In those days the font was not like ours—a basin on top of a pillar—but was usually a kind of bath, below floor level, with steps leading down into the water. First the Christ-candle was lowered into the depths and brought forth again—just as once Christ descended into the grave and rose again. Then the catechumens in turn descended into the waters as though being buried with Christ; and being washed from their sins, they arose from the font as Christ rose from His grave unto newness of life—no longer natural men but Christians, members of the Mystical Body, filled with grace, conformed to Christ in the baptismal character, destined to worship God in and through the Christian Mysteries.

By now it was early on Sunday morning, about the time when Christ, as a matter of history, rose again from the dead. How fitting, then, that at this time Christians also should rise in mystery from the death of that sin which their mystical Head had conquered, thus celebrating the resurrection of head and members together!

Arrayed now in white robes symbolic of their fresh innocence, those who had been newly-begotten in Christ were brought to the presiding bishop who anointed them with chrism and laid his hands upon them. Thus they received the Spirit of Christ, the Holy Ghost, becoming "other Christs"—for the very word "Christ" means "anointed."

Fully equipped now with the life and the powers proper to members of the Mystical Body of Christ, the new Christians singing "in the joy of their youth" went with all their brethren "unto the altar of God"; gathered around this altar, in the brightness of Easter dawn, they exercised for the first time their privilege and duty of worship by participation in those particular Mysteries of Christ in which there is to God the Father—through Christ and with Him and in Him—all honor and glory.[1]

Though we may not have experienced it all in such a vivid and inspiring manner, we must never forget the fact that all this did, in very truth, happen to us. We have been baptized—we made our *introit* into the death and resurrection of Christ; we were really—though "in mystery"—buried with Christ, and

---

[1]Readers are strongly advised to procure and study the *Proceedings* of The National Liturgical Conference for 1948. (From Liturgical Conference, Elsberry, Mo.) This volume treats more fully of the whole subject of Christian initiation, and contains, amongst many other treasures, an inspiring description—by Msgr. Hellriegel—of the Holy Saturday services.

with Him we rose to newness of life. We were equipped in confirmation with all the powers needed for full activity as members; conformed to Christ the Priest by sacramental characters, enabled to carry out our functions in the Christian Mysteries, and to be united sacramentally with Christ and with each other.

If only we realized this as we should, our minds would be filled with wonder, and our hearts would sing with gratitude to God, with joy and exultation at all these marvels. The worship of God would be for us no mere duty, but a privilege which we rejoice to fulfill. Our religion would be seen for what it truly is—"good tidings of great joy." Such an attitude would bring into its right perspective our task of living a good Christian life.

"The three sacraments of initiation," writes Dom Godfrey Diekmann, O.S.B., "the sacraments that bring us the fulness of the Christ-life, are also the sources of Christian *living*. Only because we *have* the Christ-life can we perform Christ-like actions. And *because* we have the life, we must act in a Christ-like manner. . . . How we have managed to obscure this in practice, to our very great spiritual loss! We have made of Christianity a system of moralizing—do this and don't do that—almost as if we were still in the Old Testament. Christian life becomes a matter of laboriously striving to imitate the example of Christ, a painful and discouragingly slow process, in which we are helped by the grace of God, and in which we persevere because we want to get to heaven (or perhaps, really, only to avoid hell). The emphasis is almost solely on *our* effort. And the result? Well—let us say that, by and large, it is not exactly worth boasting about!"[2]

And finally, I quote a beautiful passage from Monsignor Hillenbrand:

"The liturgy endlessly insists upon this simple truth—that the world, with all its present disabilities, is now more glorious,

---

[2]*Proceedings* of The National Liturgical Conference, 1948, p. 146.

is now more fraught with possibilities for our divine life, than paradise would have been. . . . It is idle beyond words to lament that paradise has vanished. The world is full of that lament. It is futile and self-pitying. For every regret that escapes our minds, there ought to be a cry of astonishment and delight—so far does the re-creation in Christ surpass the original divine creation in Adam.

"Doubtless one of the reasons why we are such dull, routine Christians and have so little effect upon the world is that we have no sense of this, no sense of our newness in Christ. We are so much engrossed with the riddling effects of the first sin. We sense the collapse, not the restoration. We sense the fall, not the lifting up. We sense the ancient enthralment, not the release into the new glorious freedom, the freedom of the sons of God. Our thinking is so pre-Incarnation, if I may put it that way. We direct our attention to the lost paradise, rather than to the infinitely more wonderful, though immensely more difficult, world that we now have. We live by sight rather than by faith, for the lost paradise is everywhere manifest, but the glorious world is in the realm of the invisible, the divine.

"Because of this, Christianity is not the good news, the glad tidings that shall be to all the people. Because of this, Christianity has often come to seem a burden, not a joy; a constraint, not a liberation; a disadvantage almost, not an enrichment. We lack, in brief, this tremendous sense of the newness which St. Paul says should have such a decisive influence on our lives, and for which the world hungers, never so much as now" (*op. cit.,* p. 33).

Let us all, then, cultivate this sense of newness, of freedom, of joy in our Faith, so that it may overflow into our actions and cause us, as it were spontaneously, to live holy lives whereby we may become united, ever more closely, to Christ our Head. "Let us give thanks, dearly beloved, to God the Father, through His Son, in the Holy Spirit; for when we were dead in our sins, He made us alive with Christ, that we might be in Him a new creation. Be conscious, O Christian, of your dignity! Remember the Head and the Body of which you are a member. Recall that you were rescued from the power of darkness and brought out into God's light and kingdom" (St. Leo, Sermon 1, "On the Nativity").

Discussion Questions

1. Recall the rite of baptism. What *signs* there point to the reality of our dying and rising with Christ?
2. A pagan friend claims that he worships God just as well as you do. How would you explain to him that baptism has given you powers of worship which are not part of his natural equipment?
3. What powers and rights does my incorporation into the Mystical Body give me? If I joined a labor union, would this act unite me to my fellow workers in the same way that baptism unites me with the Mystical Body?
4. Why does the baptismal character commission us to worship?
5. Early Christians received the sacraments of baptism, confirmation, and the Eucharist all at once. Discuss the manner in which their administration made a single rite of initiation into the Mystical Body of Christ.
6. I acquired active membership in a lodge after serving a period of pledgeship. Compare this with the acquiring of mature membership in the life of the Mystical Body by confirmation.
7. Show how the Eucharist completes the process of Christian initiation.
8. Christian life should be even more joyous than was Adam's life in paradise. Why do we often seem unaware of this joy? How can we increase it? List some insights into sacramental life which arouse Christian joy.
9. Christianity is often thought of more in terms of moral commands and restrictions than as sacramental life. Do you think this emphasis distracts us from a triumphant sense of our newness and freedom in Christ?

CHAPTER SIX

INCREASE OF THE BODY

A VAGUE MEMORY comes back to me from childhood days; I can't quite remember whether it was a riddle, or a game, or what, but the words of it ran something like this:

> *What are little girls made of?*
> *Sugar and spice and everything nice!*
> *What are little boys made of?*
> *Frogs and snails and puppy-dogs' tails!*

My mother used to quote it at me whenever I brought in from the garden a toad in a tin, or some tadpoles in a jar or other boyhood treasures which delighted my ten-year-old heart but nauseated my teen-age sisters—the sissies!

While the rhyme is not quite accurate, there is some truth in it. Girls and women (but also boys and men) *are* indeed

The picture. Marriage itself is symbolized by the firm grip of the two right hands; its indissolubility is indicated by the one knot made of two strands. Christian marriage is a sacrament drawing power from the Cross (in the background); it is contracted with the blessing of the Church (stole); its primary object is the generation of children, symbolized here as lighted candles because their parents bring them not only to the light of day, but also to Christ, the Light of the world.

made of "sugar and spice and everything nice." At least their bodies are made of these things. The T-bone steak which you eat today will by tomorrow have become built into you as part of your body. It is "incorporated." But not for always. Though its elements will be for a while part of your muscle or bone, they will not stay there. There is a continual process of change in every living organism; its constituents break down and in due course pass out of the body, to be replaced by others. This is called "metabolism." Those who know about these things tell us that not an atom which is part of us today was in us seven years ago.

Yet the curious thing is that we go on possessing the *same* bodies. I am perfectly sure that I have the same body that I had when I was a boy; I have even got a scar on my shin which was the result of a bad hack at football when I was fifteen. *Of course* I have the same body! Yet the whole of it has changed since then, and it has grown.

Exactly the same is true (in its own way) of the Mystical Body—the Church. It is the same Mystical Body now as the Body whose members watched our Lord ascend into heaven, whose members worshiped in the catacombs, who built the Roman basilicas and the Gothic cathedrals of Europe, and who conferred on cities and towns of America such lovely names as Los Angeles, Corpus Christi, Maryville, Loretto, or St. Paul. Those members are no longer here; they have been replaced by other members. There has been metabolism in the living Mystical Body as in all other living organisms. Unless somebody is incredibly old the Mystical Body here on earth does not possess a single member who was in it a hundred and fifty years ago. Yet it is the same Body, though it has changed completely and has grown.

What does this change, this growth, involve? It means that the same Christ is living on all the time, but He lives in an organism of continually changing members. As someone (was it Cardinal Suhard?) once expressed it, "Christ is incarnate in each succeeding generation." And, moreover,

He *grows* in each succeeding generation. Not the historical Christ, of course, but Christ as He now is, Head and Body—the "whole Christ," to use St. Augustine's phrase. He is to grow, by the continual incorporation of new members, until He reaches a certain "fulness" or "stature" predetermined by His Father.

What degree of growth that implies we cannot know—it has not been revealed to us. But when it is achieved, then the task of Christ is completed; all those whom God predestines to the sharing of His own divine happiness in heaven will have been equipped, by incorporation into the Mystical Body, with that divine life by which alone they are rendered capable of the beatific vision.

There must be, then, innumerable successive incorporations; to untold numbers of human beings a share in the divine life is to be given. But the divine life can be given only to human beings who first have natural life. Until the end of time, then—until the Body of Christ shall have reached its full stature—countless natural lives will begin, and then become elevated to the supernatural level. So that the Mystical Body needs, for the fulfillment of its destiny, powers to beget natural life and powers to elevate this life to a share in the divine nature. And God has most wonderfully provided for both.

The Mystical Body, like all organic bodies, "has many members, but not all the members have the same function" (Rom. 12:4). There are some members who have the function of begetting natural life, while others have the function of raising this life to the supernatural plane. The former are parents; the latter are priests. And, within the Body, all these perform their life-giving functions in virtue of sacramental powers conferred on them.

"For the social needs of the Church," writes Pope Pius XII in his encyclical on the Mystical Body, "Christ has provided in a particular way by two sacraments which He instituted. The sacrament of matrimony, in which the parties become the ministers of grace to each other, ensures the regular numerical increase of the Christian community, and, what is more important, the proper and religious education of the offspring, the lack of which would constitute a grave menace to the Mystical Body. And holy orders consecrates to the perpetual service of God those who are destined to immolate[1] the eucharistic Victim, to nourish the flock of Christ with the Bread of Angels and with the food of doctrine, to guide them by the divine commandments and counsels, and to fortify them by their other supernatural functions" (n. 27).

In considering the growth of the Mystical Body we are concerned, then, with two sacraments, matrimony and holy orders.

HOLY MATRIMONY

Marriage is one of the most astounding works of God's wisdom and goodness. It is perfectly certain that God could fill up the gaps caused by death in human ranks by the direct creation—body and soul—of new human beings. But instead He "created man to his own image; to the image of God he created him. Male and female he created them" (Gen. 1:27). He made human nature in some way resemble His own divine nature and the juxtaposition of the sentences in holy Scripture shows that that resemblance is to be found precisely in the fact that human beings are of two kinds, male and female.

---

[1] The English C.T.S. and the America Press translations here use the word "offer"—which could seem to imply that only those in holy orders offer the Victim, whereas the encyclical *Mediator Dei* makes it clear that all the members of the Mystical Body should likewise offer, *with* and *through* the priest (n.92f). As a matter of fact the Latin original does not say "offer," but "immolate" (*"qui Eucharisticam Hostiam immolent"*: A.A.S. 35, p. 202)—which corresponds exactly to the careful distinction in *Mediator Dei* between the immolation, performed by the priest alone, and the oblation or offering, in which the faithful should join (n. 92). Editors of future English editions of *Mystici Corporis,* please note.

How does that make man resemble God? In this way: that though God is but One, He does not exist in solitude or loneliness. He has revealed to us that within the Godhead there is companionship and loving intercourse between divine Persons. The First Person loves the Second Person; the Second Person returns the love of the First Person; and the very fact that these Persons love one another is the origin of the Third Person. The Third Person is, in fact, the personified love of the First and Second Persons for each other.

And when God created man in His own image, He arranged it that in human nature also there would be companionship and loving intercourse between human persons. He ordained that the first person (a man) should love, and be loved by, a second person (a woman); and that this mutual love of theirs should become personified in a third person—the child!

And because, in human nature, the body is the instrument through which the soul expresses itself, God made the bodies of men and women such that they could express, even in a bodily action, their love for each other. Their desire to be united as closely as possible in their love issues in a physical union by which, in Christ's words, "they two become one flesh."

And herein lies the marvel! Other physical acts of man (such as chewing and swallowing food) produce their natural result (nourishment) by processes completely within the powers of human nature (such as digestion). There is no need for any special act of God every time somebody absorbs a chunk of lemon pie! But the physical love-union of man and woman cannot produce its natural result (the generation of new human life) except by the direct and special act of God in creating a new human soul to animate the tiny organism which their love originates.

Here, then, is an astonishing action which alone, among merely human actions, surpasses merely human powers. It completely transcends nature; for it brings into play the divine power of creation! God alone can create a soul. Never, in fact, are men and women so close to God in any of their merely human actions, as in the consummation of marriage; for in this is involved both love and creation. And God is Love; and God is Creator. How wonderful is marriage, even on the natural plane!

But Christ our Lord has made it even more wonderful still. He *super*naturalized it; He made it a sacrament—one of those signs which effects what it signifies.

Remember that, as we saw in a previous chapter, the sacraments are mysterious and potent signs which are not only our actions but are also Christ's actions. They are our actions because we do them; they are Christ's actions because He endowed them with the power of making present in a new, sacramental, order of existence, those actions of His which they signify. We saw, for instance, that baptism signifies dying and rising to life. The underlying reality in the sacramental order of existence is the death and resurrection of Christ which thus becomes our death and resurrection to new life.

Now matrimony signifies union. Hence the underlying reality in the sacramental order of existence is Christ's union. It is His union, then, which becomes the union of Christians who marry.

But what is this union of Christ which, through the sacrament, becomes the union of Christians? It is the union of Christ with His Church. Christ and His Church are one. "A husband is the head of the wife," says St. Paul, "just as Christ is the head of the Church. . . . Husbands, love your wives, just as Christ also loved the Church and delivered himself up for her. . . . We are members of his body, of his flesh and of his bones. For this reason a man shall leave his father and mother and cleave to his wife; and the two shall be one flesh" (Eph. 5:23ff.).

According to St. Paul, then, it is not that Christ, in uniting Himself with His Church, gave to that union the qualities which are to be found in the union of a man with his wife.

It is the other way round. The union of Christ with His Church is the underlying reality which determines the intrinsic nature of the union between the baptized member of Christ and his partner in marriage.

Moreover, their union is not a mere imitation of the union between Christ and the Church. If it *were* just an imitation, in what sense could St. Paul say that "it is a great mystery" (Eph. 5:32)? It would in that case be no more a mystery than would the performance of Anton Preisinger at Oberammergau who, in the Passion Play, imitates the death of Christ on the cross. No; it is a great mystery because it is a sacrament—one of the "Mysteries of Christ" whereby what Christ did becomes actualized here and now in the sacramental order of existence. Marriage is thus no mere *imitation* of the union of Christ with His Church; it is that union in fact—in sacramental fact.

Thus Karl Adam can write: "The fundamental mystery of Christianity, the nuptial relationship between Christ and His Church, the fact that Christ and His Church are one sole Body, is realized anew in every Christian marriage . . . (Christian marriage) has existence only by the fact that in it Christ's sacred nuptials, His union with the Church in one sole Body, are actualized."[2]

And Dom Albert Hammenstede, O.S.B., writes: "The married couple shows forth to men a perceptible, external sign through . . . which the life of Christ with the Church is made present sacramentally."[3]

Note carefully that it is the *union* of man and wife that is the *sign;* the *union,* then, is the *sacrament;* for the sacrament is a sign. This sign is given or uttered at the wedding ceremony by the man and his bride. It is not given, but only witnessed and blessed, by the priest. Which means that it is the

[2]*Holy Marriage,* p. 10. The Liturgical Press, Collegeville, Minn.

[3]*A Great Sacrament,* p. 20. This booklet is a quite extraordinarily beautiful and instructive essay on Christian marriage, and all readers are most strongly urged to get it and study it. Pio Decimo Press, St. Louis.

man (not the priest) who gives the sacrament of matrimony to his bride, and *vice versa*.

Thus matrimony is the only sacrament which the laity themselves administer, and which properly belongs to them. (Baptism can indeed be administered by laity in certain circumstances, but it does not *belong* to them to do so.) It is thus specifically the sacrament of the laity. "It is the only one in which sacramental grace is poured forth from the fulness of Christ's humanity directly upon the members without priestly mediation."[4]

And as a result of Christian marriage man and wife become a *unit*. "They two become one flesh." This unit is a new organ of the Mystical Body—which brings into natural existence those who are destined for supernatural life within that Body. The products of its action are destined for Christ's Body and for participation in its life.

"When, therefore, a Christian man and woman unite in holy marriage," writes Dom Godfrey Diekmann, O.S.B., "they dedicate themselves to God for a holy service, the extension of His kingdom among men. They are to bring into the world not only children as images of God (every marriage has that end), but to beget adorers in spirit and in truth. Christ and the Church, His Bride, have as their first objective to form a cult-community, to praise the Father. So also a husband and wife."[5]

Surely this is an extremely important thing for parents to remember. Most parents are fully conscious of their duty to "bring up" their children in everything which regards their physical welfare. The mother is untiring in her care of the infant; she feeds and bathes him, fondles him, dresses him, takes him out in the fresh air, is ever ready to start up even in the middle of the night in answer to her baby's cry. As he grows through the crawling and toddling stage, she is ever

---

[4] Karl Adam, *op. cit.,* p. 14.

[5] *Proceedings* of The National Liturgical Conference, 1946, p. 43. Liturgical Conference, Elsberry, Mo. This whole volume is of very great interest and is earnestly commended to readers.

watchful to see that he comes to no harm. If he falls ill she will remain night and day by his bed-side to attend to his every need. And the father grudges no expense, no trouble, to see that all needed material things are supplied in abundance.

But what about the child's spiritual needs? He has got to be "brought up" to know, love, and serve God, and he cannot do this unless he is taught. Far too many parents shrug off this duty with the thought: "The Sisters will take care of all that when he goes to school." The result is that sometimes the Sisters find that a child coming to school for the first time can't even make the Sign of the Cross and hasn't heard of Jesus or Mary. There is not much prospect of a "cult community" in *that* family!

It is true that parents cannot, in practice, give to their children the entire religious training that is needed. Certain elements are beyond their own technical skill; it is for that reason that there are such things as Catholic schools. But these are meant to supplement, not replace, the educative work of parents. The final responsibility is always with them.

Now suppose you are married and have been blessed with children. You may think you can't teach them their faith—teaching is a skilled job. May be. But there are things your children can learn from you that they can never learn from any teacher, however skilled. After all, they are *your* children; you have known them intimately ever since they were born; you understand them and love them better than any teacher can do. It is God who has given you responsibility for them, and He will help you, in virtue of the sacrament of matrimony which joined you together. The instruction you have to give is not formal; you don't have to learn your catechism again and conduct classes at stated times. All you have to do is to teach them simple prayers in their pre-school days, and talk to them in simple ways about God, our Lord, His holy mother, angels, saints, the Church, the crucifix, statues, pictures, and so on.

You should always have family night prayers, when mother *and father* kneel down with the children to say the prayers together. The form of prayers should be changed periodically to suit their developing minds as they "grow in age and grace before God and men." Make them feel at home in your parish church, taking them there for private visits to explain things. Make a tour round the church, talking about the altar, the font, the confessionals, the statues and stained-glass windows according to their mental capacity. Explain the Church as "God's house," and the priest as "God's man." It is he who tells us what God says, and who sometimes makes speeches to God for us. He keeps on doing holy things in God's house. On Sundays we go to give things to God through the priest, and God gives us things back through the priest. That's what we call the Mass—when we exchange presents with God to show God that we love Him, and to learn how much He loves us. We should always be happy to go to Mass and look forward to it all the week . . . and so on. You can talk to your children much better than any teacher because you know them so well and are familiar with the way each one thinks.

Your informal conversation is actually the most important of all factors in the religious education of your children, for it has more power than any number of "lessons" in forming their outlook on life. It is the way you talk during ordinary family life, about the house or at table, which counts most. If you speak often and quite naturally about God and His power and wisdom and goodness; if you explain all joys and sorrows and problems and vicissitudes of life in terms of God's overlordship and providence; if our Lord, our Lady, the Church, the Pope, the Mass, sermons, Benediction, the feasts and seasons are frequent and easy topics of conversation in your home, then your children will learn from you the most vital of all lessons—that "God comes first." Of course, if you drag these subjects in artificially for the set purpose of impressing the children, then your talk will not ring true and they will sense it. But if God and the things of God are really the prime interest of your own lives, then they will also fill the lives of your children who will absorb their religion by the mere process of living with you. Love and live your faith in all sincerity, and your children will love and live it too. They will derive from you what no teacher, however devoted and skilled, can impart.

Tell them stories of our Lord's life; encourage them to draw pictures of anything they like, such as our Lord riding His donkey into Jerusalem, or our Lady going up to heaven. Don't *buy* a crib for Christmas, but help them to make one, however crude the result may be. Use an Advent wreath, the Epiphany blessings, and all those other customs which help to keep the family in touch with the liturgical year. There ought to be no inhibitions whatever in talking of holy things, nor any about playing "holy games" like "playing Mass" or "playing processions." Children are never irreverent when playing such games, and their powers of imagination are amazing.

I once saw a boy of eight "playing processions" with his sister of six, soon after the Feast of Corpus Christi. She walked backwards, swinging an empty tobacco tin on the end of a string. He followed her with a colored tablecloth over his shoulders and a small frying pan held, handle downwards, in front of his face. At the end of the procession, which went all over the house to the accompaniment of weird wailings with unintelligible words (how liturgical!), they arrived at the place where all their dolls and stuffed animals were arranged in seried ranks. Then he, with the utmost solemnity and deepest reverence, lifted up the frying pan and made over them the Sign of the Cross, while she, on her knees and waving her tobacco tin, uttered three times with equal solemnity the mystic words "Ting-a-ling-a-ling!" He then deposited the frying pan by putting its handle into a large flower-vase standing on the table, and together they knelt and recited the Divine Praises. Material idolatry? Not a bit of it! They knew perfectly well it was only a frying pan, but they vividly *imagined* our Lord in the Blessed Sacrament. And if ever two children were raising their minds and hearts to Him in love and devotion, it was these two. Obviously they had good parents who so filled their home with the love of God that such "games" were to these children the most natural thing in the world. It was five years ago that I saw that procession. That boy is now saying that he wants to be a priest, and the girl says she wants to be a nun. Of course, one or both may change their minds later on . . . but who knows? It is at least certain that their parents have brilliantly succeeded in turning them into a "cult community." *O si sic omnes!*

Discussion Questions

1. I have the same body I had ten years ago although the physical elements in it have come and gone. How is the Mystical Body assured a similar basic identity throughout the centuries even though its members are continually changing?
2. Christ is incarnate in each succeeding generation. Does the figure of a river with ever-changing waters give much help in understanding Christ's life in the Church? Can you suggest other examples or analogies?
3. God is both Love itself and Creator. He created man to His own image. How does the marriage union express and reflect this double resemblance to God?
4. How would thinking of the family as a reflection of the love-life of the Blessed Trinity inspire greater reverence for marriage? Is the spiritual nature of marriage meant to replace physical attraction?
5. How does Christ's union with His Church become the union of Christians who marry?
6. Does the priest "marry" the couple? Just how are husband and wife ministers of the sacrament to each other?
7. What are the purposes of the Christian family? Does our concept of the family as a new organ of the Mystical Body help us to see its purposes with a new depth?
8. Why should the sacramental concept of marriage help to reduce family quarrels, tensions, selfishness?
9. Does the sacramental nature of marriage help to explain the Church's attitude toward birth control? Toward divorce?
10. List some practical ways in which parents can help their pre-school children to grow up *spiritually*.
11. Of what value are children's stories about God and their playing processions, etc.?

CHAPTER SEVEN

HOLY ORDERS

HUSBAND AND WIFE, "they two in one flesh," form, as I have said, a new unit of the Mystical Body, having as its purpose the generation of new life. But this unit is not sufficient unto itself; it needs another in order that the final result—increase of the Mystical Body—may be attained. For its products have but natural life, and the Mystical Body lives with supernatural life.

Christ our Lord has provided for this need of the Mystical Body by means of the sacrament of Orders. In this sacrament certain members of the Body are given a special function which is also generative—they are to generate *super*natural life. They are to have spiritual offspring. That is why they are so rightly called by the title of "Father." The priest, in administering baptism, generates supernatural life in the natural offspring of the Christian spouses. Parents alone do not cause growth of the Mystical Body; priests alone do not cause this growth; *both* are needed in order that the growth of the Body may ensue. There

The picture. The functions of a priest are to offer, to bless, to preside, **to preach**, and to baptize (Ordination liturgy).

69

must be children before there can be baptisms. There must be marriages before there can be ordinations.

A beautiful story is told of Pope Pius X, that great liturgical leader who has recently been raised to the altars of the Church. After his consecration as bishop of Mantua he went immediately to see his mother. And to her he displayed, with filial pride, his scintillating new episcopal ring. She thoughtfully fingered the worn, simple gold ring on her own finger. "Yes, dear," she said, "your ring is very beautiful. But remember that you would never have had yours if I had not first had mine!"

Holy orders, like matrimony, is a "social sacrament"; it exists for the growth and welfare of the Mystical Body of Christ. Parents and priests both contribute to this; marriage and priesthood stand side by side; they both build up the Body of Christ towards its "full stature," and neither could do it without the other.

What exactly is "priesthood"? What is a priest? Something—Someone—altogether unique. For in point of fact there is *really* only one priest—Christ. There is only one priesthood—His priesthood. Before He came there were, indeed, men who were called priests. There were priests of Baal, of Moloch, of Zeus . . . but these were no more *really* priests than Baal, Moloch or Zeus (called "gods") were really God. There were also the Levitical priests of the Old Testament. They had some right to the title because their office was instituted by God, and they did for God's chosen people some, at least, of the things which Christ, the one true Priest, does for the whole human race. But their priesthood was only a partial priesthood, and it only foreshadowed the real priesthood which Christ alone has.

For the power of priesthood is the power of effective mediation between creation and its Creator. Christ alone can do that; He alone is the *Pontifex*, the bridge-builder who spans the infinite distance between God and man and leads man effectively and finally to God. "I am the way," He told us. "No man cometh to the Father except by me" (John 14:6). "There is one God, and one mediator of God and men, the man Jesus Christ who gave himself a redemption for all" (1 Tim. 2:5).

We must not think that mediation was just one of the things Christ did (like teaching, or healing the sick). He is *essentially* the Mediator; His mediative priesthood was not merely the purpose of His incarnation, but derives directly from it. By the very fact of His becoming incarnate, the bridge between God and man *was built*. After His incarnation He carried out the priestly act of offering the redemptive Sacrifice which enabled us to pass over that bridge. But the bridge was there as soon as He was here. It was not only on Calvary that He was a priest; He *was* priest from the first moment of His mortal life, intrinsically.

As St. Augustine puts it: "In as much as He is born of the Father He is God, not a priest. He is priest by reason of the flesh which He assumed."[1] The priesthood of Christ which will never have an end *did* have a beginning. And that beginning was the moment when our Blessed Lady said her *Fiat*.

"But the priestly life which the divine Redeemer had begun in His mortal body," says Pope Pius in his encyclical on the liturgy, *Mediator Dei*, "was not finished. He willed it to continue unceasingly through the ages in His Mystical Body, which is the Church. . . . Accordingly the Church, at the bidding of her Founder, continues the priestly office of Jesus Christ, especially in the liturgy" (n. 2, 3).

Thus we see that the Church—which is Christ living now in His Mystical Body—is, as He was, the "one Mediator between God and man." Christ's priesthood resides in the Church as a whole, and in every member of it. "By reason of their baptism Christians are in the Mystical Body and become by common title members of Christ the Priest; by the character that is graven on their souls they are appointed to the worship of God, and therefore, according to their condition, they share in the priesthood of Christ Himself" (*ibid.*, n. 88).

[1] *Enarr. in Ps. CX,* 3.

Moreover, as we shall see later, there is even an exercise of the priesthood of Christ through every member; all members are capable of certain priestly acts through this power which Christ has shared with them. But again we find differentiation of function among the members of the Body. Some, and those the more important, of Christ's priestly activities are carried on, not through any and every member, but only through members appointed and consecrated for that purpose. These are the "ordained."

In the sacrament of holy orders something is signified, namely, the beginning of a function of mediation between God and man. Candidates at ordination receive an office, a status, for which they are anointed. That is what they do, so it is their action. But because it is a sacrament it is also Christ's action. Hence the sacramental reality which underlies it is Christ's exercise of mediation. God the Son was not always a priest; but He began to be a priest when He became Christ ("the anointed One"). This action of His, then, becomes theirs in this sacrament, in the course of which they, too, are anointed.

Just as when men are baptized, Christ's death and resurrection become their death and resurrection, and just as, when Christians marry, Christ's union becomes their union—so also when Christians are ordained, Christ's priesthood becomes their priesthood. Theirs is not a priesthood of their own, but His priesthood made theirs by the sacrament.

A human priest is not an extra intermediary, interpolated between God and man; his mediation is but that of Christ now signified and made actual sacramentally. The priest does not say "This is Christ's body," but "This is My body." When the priest forgives sins it is Christ who forgives sins. The priesthood of Christ the One Mediator is actualized here and now in this anointed ("Christed") member of the Mystical Body. *Sacerdos alter Christus*—the priest is another Christ.[2]

---

[2]This well-known phrase must not, of course, be understood as implying any kind of "real presence" of Christ in the priest, as in the

Our Lord said He had come "that they may have life." He is the generator of supernatural life in men. He continues now to generate this life through His Church, composed of many members with differing functions. The member through whom divine life is generated within the Mystical Body is the priest. It is also his function to tend and foster and nourish this supernatural life by all his priestly activities, just as the married not only generate natural life, but also tend and nourish and foster it in all their parental activities.

"It is to the priests," says the Pope, "that all must have recourse who want to live in Christ, for it is from them that they will receive comfort and spiritual nourishment; from them that they will take the salutary remedy enabling them to rise healed and strengthened from the disaster of sin; from them that they will receive the blessing that hallows the life of the home, and the sacrament that speeds the last breath of this mortal life on its way to everlasting happiness" (n. 43).

So not only the generation of supernatural life, but also its nourishment and conservation are dependent on the priest. How essential are priests to the welfare of the Mystical Body and all its members! Yet this is a point that a great many Catholics seem to grasp only in a vague way. They take their priests for granted. They live in some parish, go to some church, receive all the needed spiritual benefits from the Mass offered and the sacraments administered there, and take it as a matter of course that if their priest dies some other will be appointed in his place. Likewise their children are taught by nuns in the parochial school; and if any nun dies or retires through old age, why *of course* some other nun will be sent to take her place.

But whence comes this priest? Whence are these nuns? The parish profits spiritually by their labours. But do they come from this parish? Almost certainly not! They originate from good Catholic homes in some other parish which, in consequence, is not receiving the benefit of their work. Yet that

Eucharist. As Fr. Charmot points out in his book *"Le Sacrament de l'Unite,"* p. 164: "The substance of man has not disappeared, nor has it been changed into the substance of Christ."

other parish needs priests and nuns. These must be supplied . . . but by whom? Surely from yet other parishes. In other words, *all* parishes which are served by priests and nuns ought to contribute their quota to the total supply. All parishes ought to be producing vocations both to the clergy and to the religious life. If they do not produce their share of vocations, then they are parasites on the Mystical Body as a whole. They are living but are not contributing.

This is a matter which parents should think about most seriously. For it concerns them most of all. Vocations come from good Catholic homes. Those which originate otherwise are quite exceptional. It is in the home that the seeds of vocation are sown; in the good Catholic home they mature; it is through ideals fostered in their homes that young men and girls go off to seminaries and convents. But such ideals will never bring forth fruit if they are not even planted. The parents, therefore, have a grave obligation to plant the seeds of vocations in their children. God will Himself make selection as to which of them He will call. He does not want *all* Catholic boys to become priests, nor *all* Catholic girls to be nuns. But surely He does want that all of them should think and pray about the idea of devoting themselves wholly to His service. For unless they do thus think and pray while they are young, none of them will become priests or nuns. And it is the business of the parents to see that the idea is put into their minds.

With boys the idea often originates from service at the altar. Catholic parents should cherish the ambition that their boys should all have the opportunity to "serve regularly and reverently at the altar—an office which their parents, however high their social standing or degree of culture, should hold in great esteem. Properly instructed, and encouraged under the watchful eye of the priest to fulfill their office reverently, regularly and punctually, these boys may well prove a source of candidates for the priesthood" (n. 200 in NCWC edition). To this suggestion of the Holy Father's I would add the further plan that all parents should strive to take their boys at least once between the ages of, say, ten and fifteen, to see an ordination somewhere. Not infrequently one sees in the Catholic papers a notice of some forthcoming ordinations; a keen and resourceful father will be able to find ways and means of securing that his sons should witness so great an event if the place be not too distant from his home.

Possibly something similar might be done for the girls. If each of them, at a corresponding period in her life, could be allowed to see the Clothing of a Nun, this might well lead to more vocations.

At certain times parents ought surely to have a serious personal talk with each of their children on the subject: "What would you like to be when you grow up?" During their last year at grade school, or a couple of years before they leave high school would be suitable opportunities—perhaps on the child's birthday. And while it is perfectly in place to discuss with them the advantages and disadvantages of careers in medicine, law, commerce, engineering, science, and so on, it would be a grievous omission on the part of a Catholic parent to neglect all mention of the priesthood or religious life as possibilities which ought also to be considered. It is sad but true that sometimes boys or girls who have derived from elsewhere (from school or from reading) the desire to give themselves to God are opposed by worldly parents, forbidden to think of such things, persuaded that to "leave home after all the money we have spent on giving you a good education" would be an act of ingratitude towards their parents. This will not happen in good homes where the children have been brought up to know that "God comes first." The other extreme, of some devout mother with unbalanced piety trying to *push* her children against their own inclinations into seminaries or convents, is not unknown; but it is comparatively rare and seldom does permanent harm because superiors discover the truth during the training period; and as soon as this comes to light the young people are advised to leave.

That brings up another point. There are some who have

tried their vocations and decided not to go on. Such should be regarded as generous souls who were willing to follow the highest vocation if God had willed it, and as sensible and courageous people who did not shrink from the quite difficult step of returning to ordinary life when they came to the conclusion that this was God's will for them. They are greatly to be admired for their high ideals, and they usually make exceptionally good laymen and laywomen precisely because they have had some more advanced spiritual training. There is many a pastor who finds that his most valued helper in the parish, the best of Catholic fathers, the keenest lay-apostle, is some ex-seminarian.

Another way to keep the idea of vocations before the minds of the children is to include in family night prayers an intention such as the following:

"O God, Who didst from eternity appoint Thy only-begotten Son to be the High Priest of the human race; pour forth, we beseech Thee, Thy Holy Spirit upon Catholic families in every land, that vocations to the priesthood may be multiplied. Through the same Christ our Lord. Amen."

The matter is so important that all good Catholics ought to pray for it anyway. The Church—which means in this context the whole body of the faithful—desperately needs an increased supply of priests and nuns because the work is constantly increasing. The more people marry and have children, the more there are who need priests and nuns. Both matrimony and holy orders minister in partnership to the Mystical Body, that it may "grow up, into a due proportion, with Christ who is the head. On Him all the body depends; it is organized and unified by each contact with the source which supplies it; and thus—each limb receiving the active power which it needs—it achieves its natural growth, building itself up" (Eph. 4:15-16).

Discussion Questions

1. How are parents and priests partners in building the Body of Christ toward its full stature?
2. A Protestant friend asks why a priest should have any more power in the Church than his own minister. How would you explain the difference?
3. Could you explain how the priest is taking the place of Christ not by his own choosing but by God's special anointing and commission?
4. In what sense is Christ both the *bridge-builder* and the *bridge* between God and man?
5. Christ alone is *the* priest. Outline the ways in which the Church, by *sharing* in His priesthood, continues His priestly office of mediator between God and man.
6. Can a Catholic who knows his dogma be "anti-clerical"? Why? Does the doctrine of priesthood help us properly to evaluate the pastor? Why could not the Mystical Body get along without ordained priests?
7. Why must an atmosphere favorable to these vocations be provided first of all in the Catholic home?
8. As parents, what prudent means could you use to foster possible vocations in your children? What means should *not* be used?
9. How many priestly and religious vocations has your parish nurtured?

CHAPTER EIGHT

THE HEALTH OF THE MYSTICAL BODY

DID YOU KNOW that the sacrament of penance (which we commonly refer to as "confession") was once a public affair? That seems rather shocking to our way of thinking, but it is nevertheless a fact. In the early centuries of the Church's history, people who wanted to have their sins forgiven went through an ordeal the very thought of which almost makes our hair stand on end. And though the things they had to do have now been discontinued, it is worth our while to learn something about them, because thereby we shall come to a better understanding of the sacrament of penance as we now have it.

Everybody knows, I think, that the low Mass is only a simplification of high Mass and that therefore to understand low Mass properly one has to study high Mass. Well, the confession we now have may be likened to a sort of "low confession" in comparison with the "high confession" they used to have, for

The picture. Christ gave to His Church the power of forgiving sins (known as "The Power of the Keys"). Sin, which is a spiritual disease in members of the Mystical Body, can be forgiven in the sacrament of penance, which is an exercise of this "Power of the Keys." (Diagram at the left of the cross.) And the sacrament of extreme unction (diagram at right of cross) heals the after-effects of sin by anointing with Oil of the Sick (*Oleum Infirmorum* in the little vessel), forgives any remaining sins (by power of the keys), and strengthens hope (symbolized by the anchor) in Christ (Chi-Rho sign).

it is a simplification—an extreme and radical simplification—of the former practice, even though fundamentally both are exactly the same sacrament.

THE SACRAMENT OF RECONCILIATION

It is queer how things often become known by names which indicate some point of lesser importance. The Mass is an instance. They say the word comes from the *Ite missa est*—the dismissal of the people, which is surely not the most important of its features! So with this sacrament—we call it "confession." Its more formal title is "penance." And, of course, it does involve both confession and penance. But the really important thing about it is that it brings *reconciliation* with God.

It seems rather a pity that we don't call it "absolution" or some such name, because that is what matters most. And that is what has remained basically unchanged throughout the centuries in spite of the changes which have come about in respect of the confessing and penitential parts of it.

In olden days this sacrament was used only for the forgiveness of mortal sins. In different times and places there were many variations of procedure and it would take a whole book to describe them all. Some points are still not quite clear and need further research by scholars. But in general it may be said that if the sins to be forgiven were secret sins they could be confessed in secret; whereas if they were public sins which the whole Christian community knew about, they were confessed, or avowed, publicly. But no matter whether the confession was secret or public, the penance was public and the absolution was public. And the penance had to be done before the absolution was given.

Terribly stiff penances they were, too—no mere "three Hail Mary's," but forty days of fasting and sitting in sack-cloth and ashes and wearing hair-shirts and making barefoot pilgrimages and all that sort of thing. Truly *schauderhaft* (or "shudder-worthy," to use a rather expressive German word)!

Let us look at a "solemn high confession" in about the sixth century. The customary (but not the only) date for this was the beginning of Lent. The entire Christian community assembled in the church, where the bishop, in full pontificals, sat upon his throne; and his priests, deacons and subdeacons ranged themselves on each side of him. The sinners were led barefoot into the midst of the congregation and prostrated themselves on the ground.

All the clergy then sang the seven penitential psalms over them, and there followed the litanies of the saints in which all the people sang the responses. Then the penitents stood up; and those guilty of public sins which had scandalized the whole Christian community (such as murder, adultery, rape, sorcery, perjury, apostasy) then publicly avowed what they had done and asked for pardon and penance. The bishop—either in person or through his penitentiary—delivered judgment as to whether pardon would be granted and what penance was to be imposed on each.

But all were treated alike in one particular (which we would do well to ponder), namely, that they were all sentenced to be excluded from the body of the faithful. All were solemnly expelled from the church, and knelt down outside the door. The bishop, standing in the doorway, then exhorted them not to despair of God's mercy, but faithfully and humbly to perform the penitential exercises he had imposed on them until the day when they were to appear before him again for reconciliation and re-admission to the Christian community. This day was usually (though not invariably) Maundy Thursday.

After the bishop's exhortation the doors of the church were shut against the penitents, and they stayed outside listening wistfully to the strains of those within as they celebrated with psalm and song the Sacrifice of "God's holy people."

The ceremony on the day of reconciliation was even more solemn. Again the sinners, barefoot and in penitential garb, knelt outside the closed doors of the church while the faithful prayed and sang around their bishop within. At one point in the service two subdeacons with lighted candles were sent to open the doors and sing to the penitents the antiphon, "God wills not the death of the sinner, but rather that he be converted and live." Later on two other subdeacons were sent to sing that "The kingdom of God is at hand." Later still a deacon, arrayed in his most gorgeous vestments, sang to them, "Lift up your heads, for the time of your forgiveness is at hand!"

The climax of all this came when the bishop himself, accompanied by all his clergy, went to the door. There the archdeacon sang to him a humble and noble petition saying that these penitents, and all the Christian brethren on their behalf, begged him to restore these members to the body of the faithful and re-admit them to participation in the communal Sacrifice. The bishop, having returned in procession to his throne, ordered that the penitents should be brought before him.

They entered the church and prostrated themselves while a psalm was sung. After that they were bidden to stand up, and the bishop himself prayed over them, singing a lovely preface of thanksgiving, something in the style of the Holy Saturday *Exsultet*. He stretched out his hands over them, imparted to them absolution from their sins, and gave them a blessing. At the end of the service the reconciled sinners were welcomed by their brethren as being again fully privileged members of the community, able once more to offer and participate by holy Communion in the Christian Sacrifice.

Now they could go home and change from their penitential garments, have a bath, cut their hair and trim their beards, and resume their ordinary clothes. And there was great joy among all the people.

What are we to learn from all this? Nowadays we make our confession in secret; we get a few prayers by way of penance; and we receive absolution, individually and at once. But we must ever remember that what has happened to us is fundamentally the same as what happened to the penitents of early centuries.

For, if we have been guilty of mortal sin, we too have been

cut off from the community; we were no longer sharing the grace-life which was our common life in the Mystical Body of Christ. We could no longer participate fully (by the Eucharist) in community worship. Our offense was not only against God, but against our brethren. He who offends the Head offends the members of the Mystical Body. Remember what St. Paul wrote: "There is no want of unity in the body; all the different parts of it make each other's welfare their common care. If one part is suffering, all the rest suffer with it" (1 Cor. 12:25).

If we have sinned grievously, then we have introduced sickness into the Mystical Body in that we ourselves have become dead members. If a man has leprosy in his hand, is he a healthy man? If he has gangrene in his foot, can he be said to be in full health? In leprosy, in gangrene—in fact in many diseases—there are cells of the body which die. And their death harms not merely the organ concerned but the body as a whole. So it is with the Body of Christ if we, its members, bring into it supernatural death by our sins.

Even if we now confess our sins privately, we must not imagine that they are private sins. There is no such thing as a purely private sin any more than there can be a private Christian. Both are social: a Christian is one who lives in the Mystical Body, and a sinner is one who has died in the Body. His sin not only damages himself—it damages the Body. His sin is not only an offence against Christ the Head, but also against the members.

Every sin, no matter how unknown it may be to others, is thus a social sin and not a merely individual sin. For it has the social consequence of harming the Mystical Body "which has many members." And "if one part is suffering, all the rest suffer with it."

The public and social manner in which this sacrament of reconciliation was once administered brought home to the early Christians a grasp of these truths much more vivid than we modern people have. We do well to think about the old ways, even if we cannot find in our hearts the generosity to wish that those ways were back again. We must not let the private manner in which the sacrament is now administered cause us to think that it is, in fact, our own private affair.

"What was visible in the life of Christ has passed over into the sacraments," wrote St. Leo (Sermon 72, 2). And Christ, in His visible life, said to the paralytic, "Son, thy sins are forgiven thee!" He said to the man who had been crippled thirty-eight years, "Go and sin no more"; to the adulteress He said, "Go, and do not sin again henceforward"; and to the Magdalen, "Thy sins are forgiven!"

The forgiveness of Christ, which heals sick members and even raises again to supernatural life the dead members of the Mystical Body, is still with us in the sacrament of penance; and a proper understanding and intelligent use of this sacrament by the members is essential for the preservation of the general spiritual health of the whole Body.

If we think again of the health of the human body in order to find illustrations of what can happen in the Mystical Body, we shall be struck with another point. It is possible for a body to be free from disease, and yet to lack strength. Suppose a man has had an operation because of some disease: let us suppose further that the operation is perfectly successful so that, after it, he is free from the disease. Nevertheless he will need convalescence before his health is again perfect. For his disease has left an effect of weakness which natural forces will eliminate.

It is similar in the Mystical Body. Even after a diseased member is cured of sin by the sacrament of penance there remain some after-effects. There is what is called the "disposition to sin"; also there may well be a debt of punishment due after the guilt of the sin has been removed. The soul is not a perfect soul, even though it be free from the disease of sin and in possession of the life of grace. There is still weakness.

And just as the natural weakness of the body, after the actual cure of disease, needs to be eliminated by natural means such as rest, careful nursing, good food, plentiful sleep—so also supernatural weakness of the soul, after the cure from the guilt of sin, needs to be eliminated by the action of supernatural means before that soul can be considered a perfect soul.

ANOINTING UNTO GLORY

Now our souls have got to be perfect souls before we can enter, with Christ our Head, into the glory of heaven. It was through His physical death that He entered into glory; so also we, the members of His Body, will enter into our share of His glory only through our physical deaths. It is then that our souls must be made into perfect souls, free from all spiritual weakness.

And Christ has left us a supernatural means designed to cause this effect. It is, of course, another sacrament—the one we call "extreme unction" because it is the last of the Christian anointings. The first anointing we receive is in baptism; the second in confirmation; some of us receive a third anointing in holy orders; but for all of us the last we can receive is this anointing in extreme unction.

The sacrament is intended, because of its intrinsic purpose, to be given to us when we are in danger of death. It gives to the soul of the sick person perfect spiritual health. It does for a soul, cured by penance of the spiritual disease of sin, what convalescence does for the body cured of physical disease—namely it causes full health and strength. Thus it completes the effects of penance, just as convalescence completes the effects of a successful operation.

And though it is a grace intended for the welfare of the soul it may, and often does, have an astonishing effect on the body. For the soul, now in perfect health and strength, may succeed in carrying on for some time longer its normal function of animating the body. The access of strength to the soul may, in other words, result in the recovery of the body from sickness.

Of course this does not always happen, for it is not the prime purpose for which Christ left us the sacrament. But it does sometimes happen; and the Church, in the prayers wherewith extreme unction is administered, explicitly prays that it may happen if such be the will of God.

What always happens in a man who receives the sacrament in good dispositions is the primary effect. His soul is freed from the after-effects of sin, given full spiritual health and strength, made into a perfect soul fit for its share in the glory of Christ our Lord. So that if the soul then leaves the body, there is nothing standing in the way of its entrance into the glory of heaven.

To many readers this will be a very surprising statement. For it cuts right across the notions which most people seem to entertain about those who die. Yet it is not contrary to any explicit teaching of the Church, and is in accordance with the explicit teaching of some of the Church's most authoritative theologians. Though indeed the Church has never defined the doctrine I have just stated—namely, that the souls of those who die after receiving extreme unction with proper disposition go straight to heaven—yet we have very sound reasons for believing it.[1]

There is no warrant for the pessimism wherewith so many Catholics seem to regard death. Many speak and behave as if they thought that nobody but a great saint has any chance of going to heaven except through purgatory.

Any ordinary person who dies will be lucky, they think, if he manages to escape hell by scraping into purgatory. There, as the result of suffering for ages in the "cleansing flames," he will gradually attain that state of soul which will permit of

[1] Quite the best short treatment of this matter that I have ever read is the paper, by Fr. H. A. Reinhold, printed in the *Proceedings* of The National Liturgical Conference for 1941. It can be obtained from Liturgical Conference, Elsberry, Mo. The volume would be worth getting for Fr. Reinhold's paper alone, even if it did not contain also much else of great value. All the best ideas in what follows are borrowed from Fr. Reinhold. But as he frankly admits that he lifted all *his* best ideas from the writings of two of my brethren, Father Kern, S.J., and Father Feld, S.J., I am certain that he will not mind my plagiarism.

his being at last transferred to heaven. This process can be assisted according to the number of Masses offered for him, and indulgences applied to him, by his sorrowing relatives and friends here below. And if he has not got any relatives or friends, or if they should forget him and have no Masses said, then he will be dependent on the "Holy Souls Box." But anyhow, provided he gets into purgatory, he will ultimately get to heaven. But that is the best that can reasonably be hoped for in the case of most of us.

Now this doctrine is sound enough except for the basic assumption which underlies it all and for which there is no proof—namely, that he goes to purgatory at all. I am not in any way denying the doctrine of purgatory—God forbid! Undoubtedly there is a purgatory, and undoubtedly there must be souls who go through it. What I am doubting is the assumption (for it is no more) that these are the souls of Catholics who, before dying, receive the sacrament of extreme unction in really proper dispositions. It seems to me that we have ample reasons for disbelieving that such Catholics (and they are a goodly proportion of practicing Catholics) ever go to purgatory at all. It seems much more probable that they leap, so to speak, out of their death-beds straight into their thrones in heaven!

This was the common opinion of theologians, almost without exception, from the scholastic age right down till the Council of Trent. From that time theologians seem rather reluctant to admit that extreme unction wipes out the debt of temporal punishment due to forgiven sin because they had to defend, against Protestant attacks, both the existence and the necessity of purgatory. They were so busy proving this that they "softpedalled" the traditional doctrine that the debt of punishment (to wipe out which is the purpose of purgatory) could be remitted by extreme unction before death.

Later theologians (though by no means all of them) have just copied them and each other. And though none of them go so far as to say that everybody who reaches heaven will do so by way of purgatory, that is the *impression* which has grown and gained practical acceptance in the popular mind.

There are weighty names in support of the alternative, older and never wholly abandoned teaching. St. Albert the Great says: "The substantial effect of this sacrament is the clearing away of whatever effects of sin there may be as impediment to immediate glory."[2] His still greater pupil, St. Thomas Aquinas, calls this sacrament *"unctio ad gloriam"* ("anointing for glory") and says: "By extreme unction a man is prepared for immediate entry into glory."[3] This would hardly be true if the anointed man were forthwith cast into the flames! Again St. Thomas says: "By this sacrament the spiritual healing of man is brought to completion, and the temporal punishments of sin are remitted, in order that nothing may remain in him which might hinder his soul from attaining glory when it leaves the body."[4]

Both St. Albert the Great and St. Thomas Aquinas were Dominicans. Many Jesuits could be quoted as agreeing with them. The most important is Suarez, who writes, after giving his reasons: "It is quite obvious that this sacrament has been instituted for the purpose of making a man ready for glory."[5] Or if you want a modern Jesuit, how about Father Capello? He says that the efficacy of extreme unction to wipe out the debt of temporal punishment is a manifest inference from the whole purpose of the sacrament. Its purpose is "perfect health of the soul for its immediate entrance into glory, unless bodily recovery of the dying man is even more advantageous."[6]

With Dominicans and Jesuits in agreement nobody could fairly say that this is dangerous doctrine!

[2]*In IV Sent.*, 1, iv, d. 23, a. 9
[3]*Summa Theol.* III. Suppl. q. 29, a. 1, ad 1.
[4]*Contra Gentiles.* Lib. IV, c. 73. See also *Summa* III, q. 65, a. 1, and Suppl. q. 32, a. 2.
[5]*Disp.* xli, s. 1, n. 17.
[6]*De Sacramentis*, II. P. ii, n. 117, n. 149.

Of course the contrary, post-Tridentine view has never been condemned. Hence those who prefer to be pessimists and to consider that a direct passage from earth to heaven is extremely rare, even for the anointed, are quite at liberty to do so. But the sacramental system left to us by our Lord certainly looks more complete and adequate, and more perfectly expresses His honor as our Savior, if we follow the older and more generous tradition of the Church.

The sacrament of the last anointing is the rounding off or consummation of the Christian life. It is the consecration of the Christian's death in Christ. Our Lord said in His own last moments: *"Consummatum est*—it is finished." The anointed Christian, as he dies in union with Christ, can make those words his own.

Death, for the natural man, is but a punishment for sin; but death, for the Christian, is the crown and completion of his mysterious, lifelong union with his Savior. It partakes of the nature of the death of Christ Himself, becoming a kind of sacrificial oblation through which he, the member, is enabled to join Christ in eternal glory. Because for him "life is but changed, not taken away; and when his earthly dwelling place decays, an everlasting mansion stands prepared for him in heaven" (preface, Mass for the dead).

He began to belong to Christ at baptism when there was infused in him the theological virtue of faith. And now he dies still united to Christ, still with faith in Him who said: "I am the resurrection and life; he who believes in me, though he be dead, will live on; and whoever has life and faith in me, to all eternity cannot die" (John 11:25). Dying now in Christ, he lives on in that eternity wherein faith is superseded by the vision of God "face to face" (1 Cor. 13:12).

Discussion Questions

1. Discuss the merits of the many titles given the sacrament of penance.
2. Recall how the early Church imposed severe public penances on sinners and excluded them from the body of the faithful until their absolution. How did all this dramatize the spiritual effects of sin and the sacrament of reconciliation?
3. What advantages in showing the spiritual realities of the sacrament did this early form of administration have?
4. Why does mortal sin damage the whole Body of Christ? Is any sin absolutely "private" in its effects?
5. Should we dread going to confession if we know its purpose? Should we go only once a year?
6. What are the various anointings received by Christians?
7. Compare the effects of extreme unction to physical convalescence.
8. What arguments support the belief that the soul of a person who dies after receiving extreme unction with proper dispositions goes straight to heaven?
9. Considering the sacramental benefits, should we wait to call the priest until someone is near death?
10. Discuss the attitudes of a pagan and of an informed Catholic toward death.

form
PART TWO
OF SACRIFICE

This is a drawing after a mosaic dating from the seventh century. It shows the institution of holy Mass. The bread and wine, by the power of Christ's consecration, become the ICTHUS (Fish), that is, Christ Himself. The fish was often used in early Christian art as a symbol of Christ because the initial letters of the Greek words for "Jesus Christ, Son of God, Saviour," when put together, form the Greek word meaning Fish.

CHAPTER ONE

THE MEANING OF SACRIFICE

IT HAPPENS that on the day I am writing this the newspapers carry exciting accounts of the great welcome which General MacArthur received in New York. Seven and a half million people cheering and waving and throwing ticker-tape! What a terrific ovation! No one—least of all the General himself—can be in any doubt as to what the New Yorkers thought about him; they expressed themselves so clearly.

That is a point worth noting—they *expressed* themselves. They did not just stay in their homes or offices or factories and think within their hearts what a fine fellow he was. They felt an interior and communal urge to come forth and demonstrate their attitude towards him. Their interior feelings demanded exterior manifestation in action. So they acted; they did what was natural in the circumstances; they cheered and yelled and waved.

The picture. From time immemorial men (such as Abel, Abraham and Melchisedech shown in the picture) have offered, as though by a natural instinct, gifts to God. Here the circle, which is a single line without beginning or end, reminds us of God's unity and eternity; the triangle reminds us of the Trinity; and the Hebrew letters are God's Name, YAHWEH. The ceremonial offering of gifts to God is called "sacrifice."

And nobody had taught them to cheer and wave. When they were boys and girls in the grade schools no teacher had taken them for a lesson saying, "When you grow up you will meet occasions when you want to welcome somebody. Now the proper way to do that is to hold your hand up and move it from side to side; and at the same time you open your mouth and shout 'Hi-ya!'" To give a lesson like that would be just about as silly as to tell children, "When you want to show you think something is funny you should emit jerky sounds like this: 'Ha! Ha! Ha!'"

Laughter is an absolutely natural expression of amusement; waving and yelling are natural expressions of welcome; they don't have to be *taught*. They "come natural"—as do many other human activities which express internal emotions. Such things are just part of human nature. If a man is angry he will frown and glare; if he is happy he will smile; if he is in pain or sorrow he will groan or weep. And he doesn't have to be taught *how* to express externally these internal emotions. Their expression is not the result of convention but of human nature.

This is true of all human beings whether they be American or European or African or Indian or Chinese. In such elementary things human nature is the same the world over. It is natural to man, then, to express externally any strong internal desires, feelings or convictions.

And there is another point in which all mankind is at one. Ethnologists tell us that there is no race or people or tribe, however primitive, which does not believe that there is some power or powers above man guiding his destiny. This is a completely universal belief. You have only to think of human history to see how true this is. Remember the ancient Assyrians and Babylonians and Egyptians and Romans and Greeks and all the gods they believed in. Think of the temples and shrines and altars of all the peoples, present and past, dotted all over the five continents. It is absolutely normal to human beings to believe in a god or gods.

Individual exceptions such as modern atheists are no more

THE MEANING OF SACRIFICE 95

against this statement than the existence of some blind men is against the statement that "man is endowed with the power of sight." Blind men are abnormalities; in like manner, atheists are abnormalities. The normal man believes in a god or gods. Whether he is right or wrong in this belief is not the point. I am only stating the fact that man does so believe.

And such a belief is, beyond doubt, one of the strongest factors in human behavior. When men believe in a god, they have feelings of reverence, of fear, of hope, of desire, of adoration. Those feelings are at least as strong as emotions of joy or sorrow, of triumph or of amusement. And just as man has natural external expressions of these latter emotions, so, too, he has natural expressions of the former. If he naturally reacts to a hero whom he admires by doing things expressive of welcome, likewise he naturally reacts to a god whom he reveres by doing things expressive of adoration. And it is very interesting to study just what man has done in this way. Let us look at a few samples.

In what is now called Mexico there once dwelt some people called the Aztecs. Quite a lot is known about them, including the fact that they believed in a god with the impossible name of Uitzilopochtli. (He wasn't by any means their only god; they had Quetzalcohuatl and Tezcatlipocha and a few other tongue-twisters!)

The Aztecs built temples in honor of Uitzilopochtli, and furnished each with a large stone slab on top of a pyramid of steps in front of his image. Sometimes, especially after a battle, they would come in a crowd to this temple bringing with them a prisoner-of-war. A man in charge of the proceedings started up some songs and dances; the prisoner was bound and put onto the stone slab; his breast was stabbed with a sharp knife, his heart was ripped out and put in front of the idol, and his body was thrown down the steps to the waiting crowd below. The people rushed at it, hacked off whatever bits they could get, and took them home to cook and eat. To us it seems a most unpleasant and gory business; but the fact remains that to them it was an expression of the worship of their god!

Somewhere in Ireland is a great monolith; the tribes who inhabited those parts long before St. Patrick went there called it Cromm Cruach and believed that it was the dwelling-place of their god. They used to come to this place in a crowd, and brought with them a little baby. They put the baby on a big stone in front of Cromm Cruach; then they walked round the stone and sang things; finally the man in charge killed the baby and sprinkled its blood on the rock and on the people. This was their form of worship!

We know a lot about the Romans—they had no end of gods, Jupiter, Mars, Venus and all the rest of them. Public worship varied to some extent according to which god was being worshiped at what time of the year; but, in general, the people came to the temple of the god concerned and brought something with them—an ox, a goat, or loaves of bread or vessels of oil or wine. There were processions and singing and burning of incense; and the thing brought was killed or burned or poured out as the case may be; and often parts of it were eaten or drunk by those who worshiped.

The Greeks also had lots of gods, such as Zeus, Apollo, Aphrodite and Demeter. Most of them were supposed to live on the top of a mountain called Olympus; and concerning their goings-on up there the less said the better! They were a thoroughly disreputable lot. But they were all worshiped in temples or shrines built in their honor throughout the towns and villages of Greece. What happened in these temples? Various things; but they can be summed up by saying that a sheep or goat or some grapes or corn or olives or oil or wine were poured out or scattered or killed or burned; and in those cases where anything was left over it was eaten or drunk by the crowds.

It would be possible to adduce scores of other instances showing how Arabs and Indians and Slavs and Mongols and Africans and Polynesians and Semites and others worshiped whatever gods they believed in, but the above examples should suffice. Always there are local differences, but always there seems to be some "least common denominator," some underlying uniformity of behavior which springs, not from the fact that the worshipers were Aztecs or Britons or Slavs or Greeks, but from that factor common to them all, namely, their human nature.

After all, there are both local variations *and* underlying uniformity even in such a thing as expressing welcome. Americans wave and shout "Hi-ya!" and throw ticker-tape. We English neither say "Hi-ya" nor do we throw ticker-tape when the Queen drives in state through London. We shout "Hurrah!" and throw nothing. But the point is that we all wave and we all shout. That is human; "Hi-ya" is American and "Hurrah" is English. But waving and shouting are just human.

Then what is national and what is merely human in all these ways of worship we have been thinking about? Whether people worship Uitzilopochtli or Wotan or Zeus, whether they eat human flesh or swine flesh or olives, whether they drink blood or wine or milk at their worship is national. But that they assemble in crowds, that they bring some object with them, do something to it, and then (often) eat and drink of it is not national—that is human. These points of uniformity are found in the behavior of all peoples; and this shows that in these things are found the completely natural expression of human worship; that to act this way when worshiping is as much rooted in human nature as is to laugh when happy or to cry when sad.

Let us now sum it up. We find that in general, when men desire to worship the god they believe in:

(a) They come together to some "holy-place-of-the-god," which is usually a stone or a rock. We would call it an "altar."

(b) The proceedings are led by a specially authorized person in charge of the worship. We would call him a "priest."

(c) An object of some kind, provided by the community, is placed on this altar by the priest; usually he does something to it (killing, burning, pouring out) to show that the community is now ceasing to possess it. There is a name for this action; it is called "immolation."

(d) Sometimes, though not always, the whole act of worship ends with a community-meal at which those present eat or drink together of whatever it was that was put onto the altar.

It is clearly (a), (b) and (c) which are absolutely needed to express human worship, for they are found in all cases; (d) seems to belong in the affair as a sort of completion or perfection because it is usually, though not always, to be found. Worship *is* expressed even without (d), though not so well or so thoroughly expressed as with it.

Now I want you to note carefully two things: firstly, that what I have written is just a description of certain *facts* about mankind. These facts are not based on the teaching of the Catholic Church, nor on the speculation of philosophers, nor on conjectures as to how men *might* express worship. They are just facts, and that's all. Man *does* express worship this way.

Secondly, just as there is a name for the peculiar noises which, as a matter of fact, men do emit when they express amusement (and that name is "laughter"), so also there is a name for the particular performance which, as a matter of fact, men do when they want to express worship. And this name is "sacrifice." If men do (a), (b) and (c), they are sacrificing. If they don't do these, they are not sacrificing. If they do these, but also do (d) as well, then they are sacrificing in a thoroughly complete or perfect manner, which gives the most adequate and satisfactory expression of their worship.

So now we know clearly what sacrifice *is*.

Our next task is to investigate what sacrifice *means*. Can we understand why it is that men do precisely this sort of thing rather than some other thing in order to worship whatever god they believe in? How are we to explain that?

We can understand it by observing that in (a), (b) and (c)—the essential actions of sacrifice—we have a particular instance of that very ordinary and intelligible human activity known as "gift-giving." We see that the community is offering a gift to its god. This is but a communal and religious form of gift-giving. So if we study gift-giving in general and understand *that*, we shall be able to understand that special and religious form of gift-giving known as sacrifice.

Why do people give gifts? They do it to express in action some message to another person. Messages can be expressed in words, of course; but the expression may be more emphatic, more forceful and complete, if it be by action. A man can say to his wife "I love you!" But if, while saying it, he gives her a fur coat or a new car, she is all the more certain that he means what he says.

What message does the gift express? That depends on circumstances, and the circumstances usually make the message clear even without any words. Suppose a man has been working twenty-five years in the office of some firm, and then retires. And suppose a present arrives at his house (a clock, a radio, a television set) with a mere card bearing the signatures of his fellow-workers in the office. Then he knows perfectly well what message they want to express. They mean "Good-bye! We are sorry you have left us—we shall miss you. We like and respect you; we hope you will enjoy the leisure of your retirement." Or suppose you are sick in hospital, and a large basket of fruit arrives with a card saying "From Mrs. Such-a-body." It is obvious that she is "saying with fruit" that she is sorry you are ill and hopes you will be better soon.

A gift, then, is a material messenger from one person to another; and the circumstances in which it is given make clear what message it expresses.

So when a community of men sacrifice (i.e., give a gift to their god) it is clear what the gift means. They are expressing in action, as forcibly as they know how, that they adore their god. "We worship you," they say; "we thank you; we are sorry if we have done things you would not like; we want your favor; we want to cement the friendship between you and us; we want to be at one with you."

Now let us observe that a gift normally carries with it a

deeper meaning than a mere message. The gift stands for the giver. A man who gives a ring to the girl he loves not only means "I love you," but also he means "I want to give *myself* to you. I want to be *united* with you." So, when men give a gift to their god they imply that they want to give *themselves;* they want to be *united* to their god. That explains why gifts used for sacrifice were not jewels or gold or silver, but human lives or animal lives or things like food and drink which support life.

Human sacrifices seem to us very horrible; yet the idea behind them is all right. It is merely that this idea has become exaggerated; a perfectly sound instinct—to give to the god that which is most precious—has become distorted. Some primitive peoples realized that human life is the most precious thing men have, and that is why they gave human life in sacrifice. Others, less primitive, realized that human life is not really theirs to dispose of, and so gave instead the life of some animal which was within their dominion. The life of the bull or goat or pig was meant to represent their own life. Or they gave things like food and drink which support human life. But the meaning was the same; they were saying in action "We want to give *ourselves* to you."

This desire of self-giving, of union, is thus truly expressed by the giving of certain kinds of gifts in certain circumstances like those of sacrifice. It shows that the purpose of sacrifice is to attain union with the god worshiped. But sometimes this expression of the desire for union goes further. Let us look at another example.

Think of a young man who has quarreled with his girl and is now sorry for his hastiness and wants to make it up. He hardly dares to call at her house because she might refuse to see him and hear his apology. She is angry. What can he do? He buys the biggest and loveliest box of candy he can afford and sends it round to her by a messenger. When she gets it she knows perfectly well what it means. He is saying by his gift, "Darling, I still love you and I am sorry for losing my temper and I do so hope you will forgive me and take me back!" His box of candy says that to her much more clearly than any mere letter of apology.

Now what happens? She knows that this gift stands for him. If she rejects it, he will know he is rejected and not forgiven. But if she accepts it, that means she accepts him and forgives him. The bond of love is forged again between them by acceptance of the present which represents him. It would be, therefore, in itself sufficient if she accepts the gift. Its purpose would be achieved by its presentation from him and its acceptance by her. The bond of love is restored.

But in practice things would hardly stop there. Knowing he is forgiven and accepted again, he comes round in person to her house. She receives him and thanks him for his candy; she opens the box and admires the chocolates. Then she does the obvious and natural thing—she holds the box towards him and says "Have one!" So he eats a chocolate, and she eats one, and offers him another and eats another herself . . . and soon they will be snuggled on a couch together with the box between them, eating *together* that which was his gift to her.

She is giving back to him some of that which is *now* hers (because she accepted it) and *was* his (because he gave it). She is sharing with him his own gift to her. And the very fact that they are eating it together draws them together still more in their love and establishes the completeness of their reconciliation.

For, even though the two of them may not think of it, there is a deep meaning behind this utterly natural action of eating together. The gift represented him, and it became hers by acceptance. Now she offers back to him this same gift, so that he too, by eating of it, may become united with it. Hence he, being united (by eating) to his present which is already united (by acceptance) to her, feels that he himself is united with her—is in *union* with her. They have a common union with the gift because they are both eating it. Thus the sharing of the gift *in common* is the final stage of the gift-giving which expressed desire for *union*. So it is called "communion"; it expresses and confirms the common union between them.

Now we can see the meaning of the communal meal which was so often the terminating feature of men's sacrifices. This meal is called "communion," and is a sacrificial banquet. The worshipers sacrifice (give their gift) because they want to forge a bond of union between themselves and their god. To show that their gift is no longer to be theirs but the god's, they make their worship-leader (the priest) put it onto the god's holy place (the altar) and do something to it (such as killing, burning, pouring out) which takes it away from them.

They feel that if their god accepts it, then he accepts them; and the desired bond of friendship is achieved. They can feel that their god is pleased with them and has taken them into his friendship.

But how can they know their god has accepted it? In some cases they just assume this. But in most cases they yearn for some sign that the friendship they believe now to exist is actually confirmed and made definite. So they look to their god to return to them some share in their own present by inviting them to "have some"—like the girl who accepts the candy and then invites the donor to "have some." The worshipers, therefore, come up to the altar and "have some." They eat of the gift which they have offered to their god, and feel now that they really are in perfect harmony and union with him. For they, by eating, are attaining union with this gift which is itself in union, by acceptance, with the god they worship.

They are united with the gift; *the god is* united with the gift; and so *they* are united with their *god*. That is what they now believe and feel. That is why the gift-giving of sacrifice finds its completion in the return of the gift that it may be eaten in common by the worshipers. By this means they attain a communal union (communion) with their god.

You will notice that all this is true and according to human nature irrespective of whether the god worshiped is real or imaginary. The men may have completely false notions, thinking that a stone is their god, or that the sun is their god or that Zeus or Jupiter or Baal or Moloch or Shiva or some other figment of human imagination is their god. That is not the point. The point is that even when the god is false, the worship is true. It is based and rooted in human nature. If men believe (correctly or not) in a god, and desire to worship, then this business called sacrifice is what they actually do about it; and they are right to do it. Because this is what they find to be absolutely natural and sincere and satisfying and adequate when they express worship.

So they offer a gift to their god. That is sacrifice. And usually they receive that gift (or part of it) back again that they may eat it. That is communion. Communion rounds off and completes and, as it were, "personalizes" the sacrifice by making it each one's very own. It is no longer just something he has watched; it is something he has done—to attain, in *common* with his fellows, that *union* with his god which he so much desires.

So far this chapter has dealt with humanity as it is—but with divinity as it is *not*. All the gods I have talked about were false gods. But they had true worship! Now let us remind ourselves that there does exist the True God—the One True God whom we are to worship. If we are to give Him true worship we can only do it by sacrifice—for that is the natural, human way of worship. And we have got a sacrifice whereby we may do it—the holy sacrifice of the Mass.

I have spent all this time in explaining the nature and meaning of sacrifice because I am convinced that an enormous number of Catholics do not understand the Mass *precisely because* they do not understand sacrifice. They know the Mass is a sacrifice because they have so often heard these words coupled together. But if one word means little or nothing, the other word will mean little or nothing too! Unless we fully grasp what sacrifice really is, it is of little use knowing the mere sound of the word.

I am hoping, therefore, that by going so thoroughly into the nature and meaning of sacrifice, I shall have laid a good foundation for the understanding of the Mass which is the subject of the chapters to follow.

Discussion Questions

1. Discuss the claim that atheists are abnormal.
2. Explain what sacrifice *is* by pointing out the common elements in the worship of peoples of various cultures.
3. Explain what sacrifice *means* by pointing out the numerous ways in which peoples have signified their giving of themselves to their god.
4. An Indian boy who was serving Mass in the mission for the first time enthusiastically decided to move the Missal a few extra times to show he was doing his part in worshiping God. How does his spontaneous *expression* compare with the participation in worship of the majority of us at Mass?
5. Another Indian child brought the missionary a jar of blueberries (half green and crushed) as her little gift because she didn't want her brother who served to do more than she did. In what ways does her gift bear the marks of sacrifice?
6. Recall examples of children which illustrate their sacrifices. Would you say it is "natural" to want to sacrifice?
7. Why is communion (sharing the gift in common) so completely natural?
8. In our culture accepting an invitation to dinner is one of the best ways of showing our friendship. Discuss how this is a sign of union. What expressions of *communion* between man and God existed in past civilizations?
9. A "sacrifice" for us usually means "something reluctantly given up" out of duty. Discuss what the term sacrifice means for Catholics when they refer to the Sacrifice of the Mass.

― Who conquered
by a Tree ―
― On a Tree
was conquered. ―

CHAPTER TWO

MAN'S YEARNING

THE NEED OF SACRIFICE

"How odd—
Of God—
To choose—
The Jews!"

Thus wrote Mr. Chesterton in masterly epigram. Odd or not, it is perfectly true! Among all those sacrificing races and peoples and tribes we considered in the last chapter, the Jews alone knew and worshiped the One True God. Zeus, Jupiter, Aphrodite, Mars, Wotan, Shiva, Ammon-Ra and all the rest of the gods—even Uitzilopochtli the tongue-twister—were all imaginary. Not one of them ever existed. Only God, our God, the True God, has been existing from all eternity. And only one nation knew of Him—the Jews. Not that they deserve much credit on the whole. They were always rushing off to worship golden calves or Moloch or Baal or others of the strange gods of their pagan neighbors.

But God would not let them alone. He had *chosen* them. When they went astray He brought them to their senses by afflicting them with a war or a plague, or with some fierce

The picture. The purpose of sacrifice is to forge the bond of friendship between God and man. A perfect and effectual sacrifice was needed because the human race had been ruined by Satan (the Serpent) under the tree of Paradise. The harm there done was repaired by the perfect sacrifice offered by Christ on the tree of the Cross.

prophet whom they found at times to be a worse scourge than either! And so they were harried and chastised and dragooned into leaving the worship of idols and returning to the worship of Yahweh, the One True God.

And how were they to worship God? In the same way as they had been worshiping the idols, of course: in the way natural to man, which is by sacrifice. God Himself told them to worship Him by sacrifices. Of course these differed in detail from the pagan sacrifices, but they were fundamentally the same thing, namely, the offering of gifts to God for the purpose of adoring Him and seeking friendship and union with Him.

In the Bible we find many stories of sacrifices offered by good and holy men—Noah, Abraham, Melchisedech and other patriarchs. And God made it clear that He was pleased with such worship. Later, when the Jews went astray and had to be brought back to Him, He positively prescribed sacrifices and laid down the minutest rules and regulations about them. Read the Book of Leviticus; read the Book of Numbers; you will find chapter after chapter filled with the instructions which God gave through Moses about sacrifices—what things should be offered, how many of them, by whom, what for, when, and how.

God was determined that His chosen people should worship Him, and that they should do it by sacrifice, because that is the only genuine, complete, natural and satisfactory manner of worship. That is why He demanded sacrifices of the Jews. And that is why He wants sacrifice from us. And so that is why we must thoroughly understand sacrifice in order that we may do it properly and intelligently. In this chapter, therefore, we will think about it a bit more. We have already discussed the nature of it; now let us study the need for it.

When men offer sacrifice to whatever god they believe in, they are wanting to forge a bond of friendship, to attain to union between themselves and their God. And in point of fact the human race as a whole was, for thousands of years, in dire need of such a bond of friendship with the True God. The first members of the human race had been God's friends and had enjoyed wondrous privileges, especially the gift of grace—that share in God's own kind of life which we studied in a previous chapter.

But alas! they disobeyed God; they threw away His friendship; they committed sin—the first, or original, sin which made them God's enemies. Hence God ceased to honor them with the great privilege of sharing His own type of life; He withdrew grace from them—they were in *dis*grace, as we say. And this had dire consequences, not merely for themselves but for all their descendants. For they were unable to transmit to their descendants that which they themselves did not have. Their children were born possessing *merely* human life, with no share in the divine life. And so with their grandchildren and all later generations. All they had was human life—nothing more.

And mere human life is not equipped with the powers needed for enjoying God's kind of happiness, which we call heaven.

Since Adam's sin all mankind (with the sole exception of our blessed Lady) came into being like that. Even now everybody starts that way; every babe that comes into this world is "born in original sin." Which does *not* mean (as so many muddle-minded folk seem to think) that the baby itself has committed any sin; nor does it mean that the baby's conception was the result of an action which was sinful. It means that the baby is only a *natural* baby, having only that type of life which is natural to human beings; it has no share in *supernatural* life which it should have—and would have had but for the first, or "original," sin of Adam.

Now if the whole human race had been left in this condition it would follow that the whole human race would be permanently incapable of enjoying heaven. All men permanently in *dis*grace—all men forever barred from heaven. What a tragedy! And what great need, therefore, that mankind should somehow regain God's friendship in order to regain grace, the essential equipment for heaven. How vitally necessary it was that the bond of friendship should be restored between God and man!

Somehow, in some obscure way—perhaps as a vague memory or tradition of primitive human bliss—men seem to have realized this. They felt, somehow, that something was wrong, and they tried their best to establish the needed bond of friendship between themselves and God by doing that which is the natural expression of such a desire—namely, by sacrificing. But they had got hopelessly muddled through ignorance and sin; they did not even know who God was; they thought God was a stick or a stone or a statue or the sun or a volcano or a being which was in fact a mere creature of their own imagination.

And so we find throughout human history all sorts of men— white and yellow and brown and black, offering all sorts of things—prisoners and bulls and goats and food, to all sorts of gods—idols and images and myths and fetishes. No doubt there was at times much evil in this idolatry; but might we not also see in the myriad forms of paganism much that was good?— the well-meant, though completely misdirected, efforts of poor ignorant men to do their best to make friends with god again?

Surely there were millions of them who were sincere. They knew no better; they did what they could; they offered worship which was perfectly genuine in a manner which was perfectly in order according to the nature which was theirs.

But, of course, they never succeeded in attaining their purpose—friendship and union with God. Why not? Because all their sacrifices (apart from those of the Jews) were offered to the wrong god—to gods who didn't even exist. And the things they offered—mere goats and pigs and bulls and corn and wine—had so little value. And the men who offered them were but poor, ignorant, sinful, limited creatures not worthy, in themselves, to be heard by the great God, the almighty Creator and Master of the world!

If things had remained like this, if all the sacrifices offered by men had failed of their purpose, then for ever all men would have been shut out from heaven. But, fortunately for us, things did not remain like this. Ineffectual sacrifices were not to be endlessly man's lot. For, through the mercy and wisdom and power of God, there came at last a day when a certain Man succeeded in offering to God a perfect sacrifice; it was a sacrifice of infinite worth which gave to God perfect worship.

To those who saw it, it looked, indeed, a ghastly failure. But it was in fact a triumphant success. Because this perfect sacrifice succeeded in achieving that which is the real object of all sacrificing: it forged again the bond of friendship between God and the human race. The days of disgrace were ended, and the days of grace began!

Of course we all know who that Man was: it was Christ our Lord, who, though just as truly man as you or I, was also God. And the sacrifice which achieved its object was the offering of His own life on Calvary. What happened on Calvary was not just the death of a man; it was a *sacrifice*. To see this more clearly let us remind ourselves of what is involved in sacrifice.

In a sacrifice some gift is offered by man to God. Some change is wrought in this gift to show that it no longer belongs to man. (This change is called "immolation"; the gift so changed is called a "victim," and the one through whose agency this change is brought about is called a "priest.")

The victim is thus offered to God. And that is sacrifice. But it is *successful* sacrifice only if God accepts the victim, uniting it with Himself. It is only in this acceptance by God that the sacrifice can achieve its purpose. But all these points are verified in Calvary.

For, on Calvary, a gift was offered to God. It was the most perfect of gifts, because it was that of a human life, the most precious thing man possesses. Normally man may not offer human life because he has not himself complete dominion over it. If he sacrifices another human being it is murder; if he sacrifices himself it is suicide. That is why for ordinary men human sacrifices are wrong.

But this case was different: here was the one and only Man

who really had dominion over His life. That is because He was not only man, but also the Son of God. He could say, "This my Father loves in me, that I am laying down my life to take it up again afterwards. No man can rob me of it; I lay it down of my own accord. I am free to lay it down, and free to take it up again" (John 10:17,18).

And so Christ our Lord did offer His human life. He made His intention of offering quite clear at the Last Supper when He spoke of His body "given for you" and His blood "which shall be shed for you and for many." He again manifested His offering in His last words on the cross: "Father, into thy hands I commend my spirit." On Calvary, then, a Man offered a gift to God.

Moreover, this gift was immolated—that is, it was withdrawn from mankind by a change wrought in it through the agency of a priest. The change was a passage from physical life to physical death. And the priest who did this was Christ Himself. He *laid down* His life. It would not be accurate to think of His death as being effectively caused by His murderers. They had no power to kill Him unless He permitted it. Nothing they could do would have brought about His death if He had willed to remain alive. It was of His own will that He laid down His life.

The immolation, then, is to be attributed to Him, and it was an exercise of His priesthood. Through His own will He became the victim of the sacrifice of which He was, at the same time, the officiating priest.

And this victim was accepted by God the Father to whom it was offered. It was a gift infinitely pleasing to Him. Had He not said, "This is my beloved Son in whom I am well pleased"? The sign of God's acceptance was the resurrection and ascension of Christ, who now "sitteth at the right hand of God the Father almighty." The resurrection and ascension of our Lord pertain to the sacrifice of Calvary as its acceptance and completion. They, in fact, constitute its *success,* namely, the union of man with God. The union was first achieved in the Person of the man who was also God—Christ our Lord.

But, as we shall see later, it involved also the union with God of all those men of whom Christ is the head—all men who are incorporated into Him as members of His Mystical Body.

So it was that, through Christ, God had at last the perfect worship which is His due; through Christ, in the Person of Christ, man had at last offered the perfect sacrifice which effected the hitherto unachieved purpose of all sacrifices, namely, the re-establishment of friendship between God and man. It made God and man "at one" again, and hence is called the "at-one-ment."

It is also called "the redemption" because it was the "buying back" of the human race, enslaved by sin, at the great price of the blood shed by our Redeemer on Calvary. Since the price was paid when our Lord immolated Himself for our sakes, it is correct to say that it was the cross which saved us and that His death was the cause of our salvation.

But we must not allow our gaze to stop there; to do so would picture our Lord's work for us *only* as a price-paying, only as a liberation from sin. It would leave out, or at least obscure, that which is far more important than this negative aspect: namely, the positive result of our being raised up to the supernatural plane by the bestowal of grace.

Not only are we freed from sin, but we are also sanctified—made holy—brought into union with God. This vital union with God is through Christ who, from Calvary, passed on by His resurrection and ascension to His place beside the Father. To think of Calvary apart from the resurrection and ascension is to think of the immolation of a victim without regard to its acceptance. The death, resurrection and ascension of our Lord all belong together as successive phases in but *one* great action—His return to the Father. This return was done in a manner such that it not only liberated us from the death of sin, but also bestowed on us new life, and at the same time it rendered perfect and all-sufficient worship to God.

With this great sacrifice everything was achieved. Nothing

whatever was lacking from its perfection. Once this sacrifice had been brought to its completion nothing could be added to it. The ultimate purpose of all sacrifice being now fulfilled, any further sacrifice would seem superfluous. That is how it would look from God's point of view.

But there still remains man's point of view; and our Lord, Himself a man, knew that man has a kind of *need* to sacrifice, since this is the natural way of expressing human worship. If there were to be no sacrifices after His, then His followers would experience a sense of frustration in their worship of God. There would remain open to them only lesser ways of worship, such as prayer.

Yet the whole of human history has shown that these lesser ways are not enough; they do not give full and complete expression to man's worship—only sacrifice can do that. If, therefore, Christ had left to His followers a religion in which there was no room for sacrifice, there would be one aspect in which it would suit human nature less well than the old, yet false, religions of paganism. Whereas the pagans could express their worship of false gods in a manner completely satisfactory to themselves, Christians, being left without a sacrifice, would have desires and yearnings which their religion could not fulfill.

Now it is unthinkable that Christ would found a religion in *any* way inferior to other religions. *Of course* Christians, being men, would want to sacrifice. Yet what sacrifice could they offer? Were they to offer bulls and goats and corn and wine like the pagans of old, even when they knew such things were futile?

That would not be satisfactory at all! Christians would want to offer a *perfect* sacrifice, for nothing else would be worthy of God. Yet how *could* they offer a perfect sacrifice, seeing that there was only one perfect sacrifice—that of Calvary?

No mere man could solve a problem like this. But then Christ is not a mere man. He is God. He has infinite wisdom and infinite power to draw on. And He solved this, our problem, by use of the "sacramental principle" which we studied previously. He offered the unique perfect sacrifice in a certain place, Calvary; on a certain date some two thousand years ago. It was then *His* sacrifice, and His alone. But by means of the sacramental principle He has overcome all restrictions of time and place, and contrived that it may now be *our* sacrifice by giving it to us to offer. He caused it to exist in sacramental form precisely in order that we may offer it.

We are not left with any second-best or obviously inadequate way of expressing our worship of God; we are not left with any mere substitute—we have *the thing itself*—our Lord's own perfect sacrifice, handed over to us in a form such that we ourselves can offer it.

For, on the night before He suffered, He took bread and blessed it and broke it and said, "This is my body which is given for you." And likewise the chalice after He had supped, saying, "This is the chalice of my blood which shall be shed for you.... Do this in commemoration of me!"

He caused His body given for us, and His blood shed for us, to begin existing in a new way—in a sacramental sign; and this sign was such that it could be available to His followers after He Himself had died, risen and ascended to heaven. It was His own sacrifice of Calvary, existing just as really as on Calvary, but not limited to that time or place. Now it has no time or place except those of the signs which signify it. His whole sacrifice was there made present sacramentally at the Last Supper. He offered it in the historical order of existence next day, leaving behind Him the command that His Church should go on offering it in the sacramental order of existence subsequently.

And that is what His Church, His Mystical Body of which we are members, has been doing ever since, on all the altars of Christendom throughout all ages and in every country to which His Church has since spread.

Therefore now His sacrifice is our sacrifice; what He offered alone on Calvary we offer daily on our altars. In the Mass we do not *repeat* Calvary; it is not that His death and resurrection and ascension happen all over again. The only thing which is repeated is the *sign* of His sacrifice. *We* do that repeating, and that is why it is our sacrifice now. But it is not a new sacrifice—it is the very same sacrifice which He offered, newly made present.

Thus it is that all that our human instincts concerning the worship of God can find complete realization. The natural expression of human worship finds utterly satisfactory realization in a sacrifice left to us by our good and understanding Master and Lord. For He knew that we would want to worship God worthily, and He left us the means for doing it.

Thus, too, it is that even from us poor and imperfect men there ascends to God human worship which is not itself poor and imperfect; for "through Him and with Him and in Him there is to God the Father Almighty, in the unity of the Holy Ghost, all honor and glory!"

Discussion Questions

1. Although they were often unfaithful to God, the Jews never abandoned sacrifice in the Old Testament. How did God insure that His chosen people should sacrifice to Him alone?
2. In comparison with the Jews, what advantages have we received from Christ to guide us in worshiping the one true God?
3. Explain how original sin affected man's ability to forge a bond of friendship with God by sacrifice.
4. The parents of a traitorous son denied him and his family any of their inheritance. How is this different from and how is it like the effects of original sin in a newborn infant?
5. Explain how Christ's death upon Calvary had all the elements of a perfect sacrifice.
6. A modern missionary in China becomes a martyr for the faith. Point out important ways in which this is different from Jesus' sacrifice on Calvary.
7. Discuss the propriety of Christ offering his own life. How does this differ from suicide?

8. What constitutes the *success* of the sacrifice of Calvary?
9. The Mass, the unbloody sacrifice of the cross, is referred to in the Canon as a memorial of Christ's resurrection and ascension as well as of His passion. Can you explain why it is necessary to include the resurrection and ascension in the prayers of Holy Mass?
10. Why is the Mass a *perfect* sacrifice?
11. Explain what makes it possible for Christ's sacrifice to exceed the normal limits of space and time and to be shared in by all of us at Mass.

CHAPTER THREE

WHAT HAPPENS AT MASS

THE MASS, as everyone knows, is the same sacrifice as that of Calvary. It is our Lord's own sacrifice, given by Him to us in sacramental form so that we may offer it "through Him and with Him and in Him," thus giving to "God the Father in the unity of the Holy Ghost all honor and glory." The Mass is the same sacrifice as that of Calvary because it is offered by the same High Priest, Christ Himself; it has the same Victim; and it is offered for the same purpose—the glory of God and the sanctification of men.

On Calvary the immolation of Christ was accomplished in visible blood-shedding; it was located in that place and happened at that particular time. But in the Mass the very same reality is there, but it exists in the sacramental order of "effective signs" instituted by our Lord. Wherefore it is not now

The picture. The Christian Sacrifice is Calvary (the Cross) made present in the offering of the Bread and Wine consecrated into the Victim of Calvary by the priests of the Church and offered to God in sacrifice by them and by all the faithful.

visible to us—only its "sign" is visible. And its location and date are those of its signs—in Rugby, England, on April 27 or in St. Louis, Mo., on September 8, as the case may be. It is no longer limited to Jerusalem, Palestine, on the 14th Nisan, A.D. 33 (or whatever the original date may have been). These differences are known, I think, to everybody.

But now I want to direct the attention of readers to another difference between Calvary and the Mass: one which is not so frequently considered and yet which is of enormous importance to all of us. It is vitally necessary that its consequences be appreciated, especially by the laity. The difference I refer to is this:

On Calvary Christ offered sacrifice *as He then was*. But at Mass Christ offers sacrifice *as He now is*. "Christ as He then was" had but His physical body as the instrument of His activity. But "Christ as He now is" has a Mystical Body through which He now acts. Therefore on Calvary He sacrificed in His physical body, but at Mass He sacrifices in His Mystical Body. "And you are Christ's Body, members of it," as St. Paul tells us.

Whence it follows that you, the laity, offer the Sacrifice of the Mass, because Christ is offering it through you, His members. That is one of the most important truths which the liturgical movement has brought into prominence. At Mass you, the laity, are *offering sacrifice*. You are not just watching a sacrifice being offered by the priest at the altar. Nor is it merely being offered for you, even at your request or with your approval, in your presence. You yourselves are offering it with and through the priest. Together with him, you are sacrificing.

Now that statement cuts right across the idea which seems to have taken root in the minds of many people. They vaguely feel that the offering of the Mass is the priest's business; he does it all; it is *his* affair. Their business is to be present, to watch, to approve, to take an interest, and to say what prayers they can while the priest gets on with *his* business, which is his concern even though he be doing it for them and on their behalf.

Of course there are those who help the priest, such as the server who moves his book about and carries cruets to him; at sung Masses there is a choir which renders incidental music, and a lot more servers who carry thuribles and candles to make things more impressive and intensify the "religious atmosphere." But even so, it is the priest's function to offer sacrifice, and his alone. The laity are but prayerful spectators.

It is lamentable that such ideas have become common, for they are wide of the truth. What, then, is the truth of the matter? It is that the laity are not just spectators of the Mass, but that they truly *offer* the Mass with the priest.

But is not the Mass a sacrifice? And is not offering sacrifice a priestly act? Yes, indeed! Then how can the laity perform a priestly act? They can do so because they all share, according to their degree, in the priesthood of Christ. And the power which comes to them in this share (called by Pope Pius XI "the priesthood of the laity") is the power to offer sacrifice.

Then if the laity, in virtue of their lay-priesthood, can offer sacrifice, what need is there of the clergy? The answer is that though lay-persons can indeed offer sacrifice, they can only do this if there be a sacrifice for them to offer. And they cannot produce a sacrifice. Only an ordained priest can do that.

Perhaps an example may make this clearer. I can eat lemon pie. Undoubtedly I possess the powers required for this delectable activity. But I can only eat lemon pie if there be a lemon pie for me to eat. And I cannot produce one for I am no cook. I need a cook to make one for me; and then I can eat it.

Likewise you of the laity, in virtue of your share in Christ's priesthood, can offer sacrifice. You have the powers required for this activity. But before you can actually do it, you need one of us ordained priests to provide the sacrifice you and we are to offer. That is what we are for; that is our highest function and privilege. For we have more of Christ's priestly power than you have. We can place upon the altar before you the very sacrifice of Christ, in sacramental form, that you may offer it with us and through us. But without one of us to do this for you, you cannot offer sacrifice.

But though we have this power, we cannot impart it to anyone else. It needs a still greater share in the priesthood of Christ to do that; it needs what is called "the fulness of the priesthood" which is possessed by the bishops. They not only have, but can also transmit to others, the power to produce sacrifice. That is what they do when they ordain priests.

All priestly powers come from Christ, for He alone is the great High Priest of the human race. He is the "one mediator between God and men"; His is the only real priesthood. But He lives on now in His Mystical Body, which, in consequence, possesses and exercises Christ's priesthood. "But not all members have the same function." Different shares in this priesthood are communicated to different members. There are, as it were, three grades of the priesthood, each having more priestly power than the one below it.

The first, or basic, power of the priesthood is that of *offering* sacrifice. Though shared by all members, they possess and exercise it in different ways according to their rank.

The second is the power to *produce* or make present the sacrifice of Christ, thereby offering it. This is the power to consecrate; it is given only to those who are ordained priests, and might be termed "the priesthood of the clergy."

The third is the power to *transmit* consecrating-power—that is, the power to ordain priests. It is given only to those who are bishops and is known as the "fulness of the priesthood."

All these are priestly powers, and all those who have them are sharers of the priesthood of Christ. The point for you laity to note is that you have the first of them. You share in Christ's priesthood because you are members of Christ the priest. That is what Pius XII said in his encyclical on the liturgy, *Mediator Dei:*

"By the waters of baptism, as by common title, Christians are made members of the Mystical Body of Christ the priest; and by the character which is imprinted on their souls they are appointed to the worship of God. Thus they participate, according to their condition, in the priesthood of Christ" *(Mediator Dei,* n. 88).

Thus wrote Pope Pius XII in his famous encyclical. Yet he is only saying, in a different way, what the first Pope said in his first encyclical. St. Peter was the first pope; and his First Epistle was thus the first papal "encyclical." In its second chapter we find: "You are now a holy priesthood, able to offer up that spiritual sacrifice which God accepts through Jesus Christ." (What can St. Peter mean by this, if not the Mass?) "You are a chosen race, a royal priesthood, a consecrated people, whom God means to have for himself" (1 Pet. 2:5, 9).

You see, then, that Pope Pius XII, in teaching you that you share Christ's priesthood, is but repeating what the first Pope taught to his flock. And Pius XII exhorts you in burning words:

"It is most important for all the faithful to understand that it is their duty and highest privilege to take part in the eucharistic Sacrifice.... Let the faithful learn to what a high dignity they have been raised in the sacrament of baptism" *(Mediator Dei,* nos. 80, 104).

Your highest dignity, then, is your "lay-priesthood." And you can exercise its powers in the priestly act of offering the holy Sacrifice of the Mass. With what enthusiasm and joy you should welcome every opportunity of doing this! How delighted you should be at every chance of assisting at Mass, not merely when you are bound to do so, but every time it is possible to go freely. But to appreciate all that is involved in this we must discuss yet another consequence of your membership in the Mystical Body of Christ.

It is a consequence which comes to light through that same difference between Calvary and the Mass we referred to above. For Calvary, precisely because it was a sacrifice, was the offering of a victim to God. And that victim was Christ Himself. And the Mass, as a sacrifice, is likewise the offering of a victim to God. And it is the same Victim—Christ Himself.

But on Calvary Christ offered Himself as He then was—possessing only His physical body. And in the Mass He offers Himself as He now is: and now He has a Mystical Body. "And you are Christ's Body, members of it." Therefore in the Mass you are offered; you are victims! And as you are offering, it follows that you must offer yourselves.

How are you to do this? Merely in words? No!—that would be prayer rather than sacrifice. Sacrifice is an action—the giving of a material gift. You therefore offer yourselves by giving a gift.

Let us think again about gifts. A gift has two aspects—its value and its meaning. A rich young man gives to the girl he loves a platinum engagement ring blazing with many diamonds. A not-so-rich young man gives to his girl a thin gold ring with no diamonds in it. The first ring is far more valuable than the second, yet both have the same meaning. Both rings mean "I want to give myself to you." So meaning is not the same as value. Very often meaning is far more important than the value—which may be little or nothing. Another example will show that.

Suppose there is a little girl—say of four or five—who observes her father give to her mother a birthday present at breakfast. It's Mommy's birthday! Then she too will want to give her Mommy a birthday present. What can she do? She wanders out into the garden and there the bright glow of a dandelion catches her eye. It is only a weed, really; but she does not know that. To her it is a pretty flower. So she plucks it and toddles into the house and gives it to her mother as a birthday present.

The mother, of course, is delighted. Why? Does she want a dandelion? Obviously not for itself—it has no value. But it is a gift from her daughter; and precisely because it is a gift it is also a *sign*. It signifies—it has a *meaning*. It means the love of that little girl, and *that* is why it is precious to the mother. Clearly, then, a gift which is poor in value can be rich in meaning.

And so it is with us and God. We give Him a present. In itself this present consists of a round bit of unleavened bread and a cruet of wine—a very small value! But because it is a gift it is a sign. It *signifies:* it bears the meaning we put into it. We should, then, make it mean all that we can in the way of adoration and love; we should put *ourselves* into that bread and wine just as the child put herself into the flower. Then it will be precious to God as the flower was to the mother.

That is the purpose of the offertory at Mass. The priest holds up first the bread on the paten, and next the wine in the chalice. And he tells God what we intend them to mean. Now you laity are helping to offer the sacrifice, so it is your business at that time to tell God what those gifts—which are *your* gifts—are intended to mean as far as you are concerned.

They mean *you.* You put yourself onto that paten with the altar-bread, offering to God your mind and heart, your soul and body, all that you have and are. You must, as it were, pour your heart out into that chalice, and put therein all your hopes and fears, your joys and sorrows, your love and adoration— your whole self. For all this is to go to God in the shape of your gifts.

That is your part at this point in the sacrifice: you are to put the meaning into the gifts by offering yourselves. If you do not offer yourselves to God under these symbols of bread and wine then you are not offering your Mass properly. You are not "in on it." The bread and wine may mean somebody else—your neighbor, perhaps, who is offering himself as well as he knows how. But they don't mean *you* because you haven't done anything to make them mean you. Instead you have been doing something else—mooning about and daydreaming, or praying to St. Anthony for something you have lost, or just saying a lot of "Hail Mary's" because you feel you ought to be doing something.

Certainly you ought to be doing something—but not *that.* At least, not at the offertory during Mass. If you want to pray to St. Anthony or say "Hail Mary's" by all means do so—but at some other time, not during the Mass. Because now, at the offertory, you ought to be telling God that these gifts on the altar are your present to Him, that they mean *you*, that you are offering *yourself* through them.

You can, of course, tell God this in your own words if you like. That would be excellent; it might suit you personally better than any other way. But you might find it easier to use some words which have already been composed to express what you mean—such as those found in "Devotions for Mass: The Offertory" out of some prayerbook. But there happens to be a book in which all this is expressed more perfectly than in any prayers you could make up on the spur of the moment, and more beautifully than in "Devotions for Mass." That book is the very book which the priest uses at the altar—the Church's own book, called the missal. It is the finest book of all. The Pope says:

"The faithful must not be content to take part in the eucharistic Sacrifice by the general intention which all the members of Christ and the children of the Church ought to have; they ought also, in the spirit of the liturgy, to unite themselves closely and of set purpose with the High Priest and His minister on earth" *(Mediator Dei,* n. 104).

You cannot unite yourself more closely with the priest than by using the very same words at the very same time. It is hardly possible, then, to improve on the missal.

But, of course, you are not bound to use the missal prayers. Only the priest is bound to them. All that is essential as regards you is that you should be doing the right thing with your mind and will at the right moment; that is, at the offertory you should be putting the meaning into the gifts; you should be offering yourself to God. If you are not doing that, but something else, then you are not doing the right thing. You are distracted from the Mass.

But now let us suppose that everybody is doing his or her part properly. Everybody puts meaning into the gifts. As a result they become, in God's sight, something of real importance, something truly welcome to His divine Majesty. For they are the expression of our worship and self-dedication. Surely God is pleased with that!

Undoubtedly. But still, we must remember that however much *meaning* these gifts may have, they are still without value. They are only a bit of bread and a few drops of wine. On the altar we have got something which is the best we can do—our gifts mean a lot indeed. But in themselves they do not amount to much. If that is all we can do, we have not gotten very far with our desire to offer to God a completely worthy gift expressive of perfect worship.

Yet, of ourselves, that is just about all we can do. Fortunately, however, we are not left to ourselves. For we are not mere individuals; we are not just Tom and Dick and Peter, not just Mary and Jane and Anne; we are members of the Mystical Body at worship. And we have a Head. Our Head, though He is one of us because He is a man, is also God. And the Mass is His sacrifice as well as ours. So He comes to our rescue. He uses His divine powers to turn our poor gifts into His.

For, although *we* can do no more, once we have put the meaning into our gifts, *He* does not have to stop there. He does for us, His members, what we cannot do for ourselves; He puts value into our gifts. From a comparatively worthless bit of bread and wine they become the infinitely precious body and blood of Christ.

This, of course, is what happens at the Consecration. Our Lord makes this wonderful change for us by using as His instrument one of those members of His Mystical Body to whom has been given the power to consecrate—one of us ordained priests. You "lay-priests" have no part in this at all. You can but believe and admire. You, at this point, are spectators and not agents. We are agents: we do the consecrating. Not, indeed, by any power of our own, but through Christ's power operative in us. We, so to speak, lend Him our mouths to say the words and our hands to hold the gifts. We are active and you are not.

But as soon as we have consecrated, you become active again. We all now have the same activity—that of offering. There lie our gifts on the altar—but what gifts they are now! They are full of meaning because we put the meaning into them at the offertory. And they are infinite in value because Christ our Head put the value into them at the Consecration. They signify all of us, both Head and members, offered wholly and completely to God. Indeed, as regards our Head, they do more than signify—for they *are* Christ whole and entire, just as He was on Calvary.

So now, both as regards meaning and value, our gifts are perfect gifts through which we offer to God perfect worship.

That, then, is what we do. As our sacrificial Victim is now there on the altar, we sacrifice—we offer the Victim to God. All of us exercise our priesthood "according to our condition." You, the lay-priests, offer this victim to God. Father So-and-so, the ordained priest, offers this Victim to God. Christ the High Priest offers this Victim to God. So that "through Him and with Him and in Him there is to God the Father Almighty, in the unity of the Holy Ghost, all honor and glory!" *That* is what happens at Mass.

Hence when the divine Victim has been placed upon the altar it is your business to offer It. Your minds and your wills, as soon as the Consecration is effected, should be occupied with this activity—offering the Victim to God. You should not be engaged in any other activity, not even (except as a kind of secondary advertence) in adoring Christ really present. You are not at Mass primarily to adore Christ, but to offer Him. It is to Benediction that you come to adore Him; at Mass you *offer* Him, in order to adore the Father. The more closely you attend to this offering of Christ, so much the more perfectly do you worship the Father.

You can offer Him in any way you like—in your own words or in the words of some prayerbook; but the best of all words to express this offering are found in the missal. Certainly you are not bound to use these words—but just look at them now and see how exquisitely fitting they are:

"Wherefore, O Lord, we Thy servants, and with us all Thy holy people, calling to mind the blessed passion of this same Christ Thy Son, our Lord, likewise His resurrection from the grave and glorious ascension into heaven, offer to Thy sovereign majesty, out of the gifts Thou hast bestowed upon us, a sacrifice that is pure, holy, and unblemished, the sacred Bread of everlasting life, and the Cup of eternal salvation."

"Humbly we ask of Thee, God Almighty, bid these things be carried by the hands of Thy holy angel up to Thy altar on high, so that those of us who by partaking of the sacrifice of this altar shall have received the sacred body and blood of Thy Son, may be filled with every blessing and grace; through the same Christ our Lord."

"Through whom all these good gifts created by Thee, Lord, are by Thee sanctified, endowed with life, blessed and bestowed upon us. Through Him and with Him and in Him, Thou, God almighty Father, in the unity of the Holy Spirit, hast all honor and glory, world without end, Amen."

Can anybody imagine a more perfect expression of precisely what we are doing and why we are doing it? And if you may use these lovely words, what adequate reason is there for using any others? Nothing but the best should be given to God; and here, in the missal, is the best! But whether you do it in these best words, in inferior words, or with no words at all, see to it that you do *the right thing* and not some other thing; see to it that you *offer the Victim to God*. Then you are sacrificing properly, making correct and intelligent use of that share of Christ's priesthood which is yours.

Discussion Questions

1. What is the same and what is different in the sacrifice of Calvary and in the Mass?
2. What evidence from the Mass prayers can you find to show that Christ, in offering sacrifice *as He now is,* makes us co-offerers of the Mass?

3. There is only one priest by nature—Christ. How do the baptized, the priests, and the bishops share in different ways in His priesthood?
4. How did St. Peter express the truth of the priesthood of the laity? How might our appreciation of this truth affect our participation at Mass?
5. The Mass is worship of the Father through the offering of Christ as victim. Explain the different ways in which the laity as lay-priests, the ordained priest as celebrant of the Mass, and Christ as the High Priest offer this Victim to God.
6. Give a few examples of how a gift poor in *value* can be rich in *meaning*. Why is the Mass the greatest case of this?
7. In earlier times the faithful demonstrated in a very active way that their offerings of grapes and bread and olives stood for themselves. How can the modern-day Catholic make the bread and wine signs of his co-victimhood with Christ?
8. What can a person like yourself offer at Mass?
9. The essential thing for us is to put meaning into the gifts we offer. How do the following prayers said during Mass rate in helping us in our offering—the Morning offering, Rosary, Memorare, Missal prayers?
10. In Mass the bread and wine as gifts of little meaning and practically **no value become rich in meaning** and infinite in value. Describe how this action takes place.
11. How do Mass and Benediction differ as kinds of prayers?
12. Why is the Church wise in requiring Sunday Mass attendance although all other special forms of worship are optional?

CHAPTER FOUR

COMPLETING THE SACRIFICE

THUS FAR we have attempted to see clearly that the Mass is a sacrifice, a particular form of gift-giving which is in full accordance with our way of dealing with each other, and so also with almighty God. It is not just a prayer, but an action. It is not just any action but this particular action of gift-giving.

We give our gift to God; like all gifts, it has a meaning and a value. Our gift starts off as bread and wine, having little meaning and practically no value. We put the meaning into it at the offertory and Christ puts the value into it at the Consecration; and then all of us—Christ and we—offer the now perfect gift, rich in meaning and infinite in value, to God our Father in worship. And that is the sacrifice of the Mass.

But is that all of the Mass? No! It would not be natural if that were all there is to it. Our human nature needs more. Think again of the instances of gift-giving we have taken as examples—the young man who gave his girl a box of candy, and the child who gave her mother a flower. What happens in these cases? Is everything complete when the gift has been given? Not at all! There is a return-gift, and so an *exchange of gifts*. That is what is natural. And is there only action? Only giving?

The picture. The form under which Christ (left panel) perpetuates His Sacrifice (Lamb that was slain) in His Church is that of a banquet (table laid for a meal, with couches in front of it for the guests) to be distributed by His priest (right panel).

Again, no. There is also conversation—a preliminary *exchange of words.*

Look at one of the examples in detail: the young man, the girl and the candy. It would not be natural for him to appear before her in silence holding his box out to her; nor would it be natural for her to take it without a word. First of all there is some conversation. He says "Hello, darling! I've brought you a present and I hope you'll like it." And she replies "What is it? OO-o-o-oh! How marvelous! You are a perfect dear to have thought of it!"—or something like that. They begin by making *verbal* contact with each other; they *exchange words.* That is the natural prelude to gift-giving.

And what next? He gives the box; she opens it and eats some. Does she then put the lid on and stow it in a cupboard? Not likely! When she has tasted the candy, the obvious and natural thing is to offer some to him, so that he, too, may eat. He gives to her—so she gives to him. That is what "comes natural." They *exchange gifts.*

And it is just the same with us and God. We come to give God a gift. We don't just do it in silence—we begin by making verbal contact with God. We call out to Him. We say (equivalently), "Dear God, have mercy on us" *(Kyrie eleison).* We say, "God, how wonderful you are! *(Gloria in excelsis Deo* . . .)." We say, "Please, God, we want something! *(Oremus. Deus a quo bona cuncta procedunt* . . .)." Thus we send our words up to God.

And then God replies. He sends His words down to us. He speaks to us through one of His apostles or prophets *(Lectio epistolae beati Pauli Apostoli* . . .). Then He speaks to us through His only-begotten Son, our Lord *(Sequentia sancti Evangelii secundum Joannem* . . .). Sometimes He speaks to us also through His minister, the priest. Thus we hear the epistle, the gospel and the sermon—each called "the word of God."

How simple and how natural all this is: our words go to God *(Kyrie, Gloria, Oratio),* and then God's words come to us *(epistle, gospel, sermon).* What is all this but *exchange of words?*

Now we proceed to our gift-giving. We hold out (in the hands of our priest) our bread and wine. We put the meaning into these gifts (offertory). Christ puts the value into the gifts (Consecration). And then we all offer them to God, through Christ and in Him and with Him. Our gift goes to God.

But is that the end of the proceedings? Does nothing else happen? It would be very unnatural if that were so. If the young man who gave a present to his girl gets something back, if the child who gives a present to her mother gets something back, shall not we who have given a present to our God get something back?

Of course we do! God offers back to us a share of what we gave to Him, just as the girl offers back to her swain a share of what he gave her. God says "Have some!" And so we come to the altar and eat of the sacrificial gift. That is Communion. It is the return-gift from God—the natural and obvious sequel to our giving a gift to Him. *Exchange of gifts!*

See now the whole outline of the Mass; see how simple it is and how utterly natural.

First, *exchange of words.*

Our words go up to God *(Kyrie, Gloria, Oratio).*

God's words come down to us *(epistle, gospel, sermon).*

Second, *exchange of gifts.*

Our gift goes up to God *(offertory, Consecration).*

God's gift comes down to us *(Communion).*

Thus the whole process is complete.

Holy Communion, then, is an integral part of the Mass. It belongs in the Mass. It is not something on its own—a sort of extra to be put in or left out or put before or put after Mass according as people happen to be feeling pious or cold or hurried or leisured. It belongs *in* the Mass and *to* the Mass and is *part of* the Mass.

Now nothing is complete if any of its parts are missing. The Mass is sacrificial worship not merely of the priest, but also of the people. And Communion is part of it. So if people leave out their Communion at Mass they are leaving their sacrificial worship somehow incomplete. They have not "finished the job." They have made no *exchange* of gifts with God.

It is true, of course, that people are not individually bound by any obligation to complete this exchange; but in order to ensure that there shall be an exchange the Church insists that God's return-gift shall always be accepted by somebody. And that "somebody" is the priest who is bound to receive Communion at every Mass which he celebrates.

But what about the people who offered the sacrifice "according to their degree" with him and through him? Surely it is not seemly or proper or natural or reasonable if they, who have given a gift, refuse to accept God's gift in return? On the contrary. Even if it is not of obligation for them, it is "right and just, proper and salutary"—and also reasonable and natural—that *all* those who offer should likewise receive. In other words all should go to holy Communion at every Mass.

For it is by communicating that each person really appropriates, makes his own, "personalizes" the Mass he has helped to offer. It is the most important of all possible ways of sharing in the sacrifice. Not only does common sense make that clear, but even the very words used in offering the sacrifice imply it. For, just after the Consecration, when the Victim is there to be offered, the priest in the name of all prays: "We humbly beseech Thee, almighty God . . . that as many of us as shall partake from this altar of the most sacred body and blood of Thy Son may be filled with every heavenly blessing and grace."

Don't people want to be filled with every heavenly blessing and grace? If they do, they should "partake from the altar of the most sacred body and blood" of God's Son. If they do not so partake, then they will not be "filled with every heavenly blessing and grace." Doubtless they will receive some blessing and some graces, for they have worshiped God and offered Him their gift.

But unless they also receive God's return-gift in holy Communion they will not have derived from their sacrifice all that they might have done. If they miss holy Communion they miss the most precious grace and blessing of all!

That, then, is the ideal, the right and proper and reasonable thing—that everyone who offers the Mass should receive holy Communion thereat. If there are five people besides the priest at Mass, there ought to be five Communions. If there are fifty people, there should be fifty Communions. If there are five hundred people, there should be five hundred Communions. If there are only four hundred and ninety-nine Communions, then some member of that worshiping community has spoiled the perfection of the worship by not fully doing his part; somebody has omitted his gift-exchange with God.

In case anyone thinks I am urging some new and startling doctrine, I would point out that this was the invariable practice of the early Church. People in those days seem to have understood far better than modern folk what the sacrifice of the Mass involves. Nobody then would think of offering Mass without receiving Communion. Everybody always communicated (unless he had been *ex*communicated; which meant not only that he was debarred from communicating—that is, from receiving God's gift—but he was not allowed either to sacrifice—that is, to offer his gift with his brethren).

It is very sad that, for a variety of reasons which for lack of space cannot here be described, people in the course of centuries became ignorant and slack. Fewer and fewer received holy Communion at Mass. At last things got so bad that the Fourth Council of the Lateran, in 1215 A.D., had to make a law that people *must* receive holy Communion at least once a year. To such a low ebb had Catholic devotion sunk by that time!

About three and a half centuries later, in 1562 A.D., the Council of Trent tried to make people see the ideal again. The Council taught that it was desirable "that at every Mass the faithful present should communicate, not only by spiritual desire, but by actual sacramental reception of the Eucharist."[1] So that is the official teaching of the Church.

[1] Session XXII, chap. 6. Denziger *Enchiridion,* n. 944.

Yet one would hardly think so, judging by the behavior of lots of Catholics at Sunday Mass. Go into any church on Sunday morning and watch! At the earlier Masses there are many who do things properly, exchanging not only words, but also gifts with God. They do partake of the sacrifice by holy Communion. But even at these Masses there are usually a number who spoil the perfection of the community worship by not communicating. At later Masses things get bad; and the last Mass is often shameful. There may be hundreds of people in a packed church, yet nobody (or almost nobody) at Communion.

Truly that is a shocking sight; it betrays widespread apathy and ignorance of what the Mass is and what it means. For reason, the words of the Mass and the official teaching of the Church all tell us that the ideal is for everybody at Mass to receive holy Communion as their part of it.

Yet all these hundreds (or thousands or millions if we think of the whole world) are falling short of that ideal. The Mystical Body of Christ as a whole, instead of being "filled with every blessing and grace," is being undernourished, because vast numbers of its members, even though they avoid mortal sin by being present at the sacrifice, show no appreciation of the return-gift of the sacrifice which God offers to them.

Why do they do it? As I have said, it is through apathy and ignorance. It is apathy in the case of those who come to Mass merely because it is of obligation. They are there just because they have got to be there. They are doing the absolute minimum consistent with not lapsing from the faith. They are bound to come to Mass, so they come. They are not bound to receive Communion, so they don't. They are not concerned to please God and give Him glory—they are concerned only to escape hell. What an attitude! They are not much use to the Mystical Body!

But I am convinced that there are others with better dispositions than that, who nevertheless refrain from Communion. And in their case it is not so much apathy as ignorance. They do not fully realize that Mass and Communion belong together. Instead they have got from somewhere or other a different idea of what things "belong together," and it is a wrong idea. For they connect Communion with confession rather than with the Mass. They think that confession and Communion belong together in such a way that one connotes the other; they imagine that you may not normally go to Communion unless you have first been to confession—that confession is necessary before each Communion.

This idea is wrong. It is the remains of a heresy called Jansenism, which was condemned about three hundred years ago. Yet its effect persists in this form. The idea is wrong, and it has bad effects.

It is wrong: because the truth is that confession is a necessary prelude to holy Communion *only* for those who are in the state of mortal sin. If they are not in mortal sin, they need not go to confession. (Of course they may, if they like, but I am here speaking of *obligation*.) They can—and should—receive Communion at their Mass even if they have not recently been to confession.

Imagine yourself up in the choir-loft of some church on a Sunday morning; you look down on hundreds and hundreds of Catholics at Mass, and you observe that only half of them (or less, if a late Mass) go to Communion. Can you really believe that all the rest are in the state of mortal sin? Is the church half-filled with God's enemies—people who have done something so wicked that they are hanging over the pit of hell? I can't believe that of them!

I think the explanation is merely that they are people who do not happen to have been to confession the previous evening, and that they therefore consider themselves unworthy to communicate. Those who do communicate are those who went to confession yesterday; those who do not communicate are those who did not confess yesterday. That, I think (apart from the exceptions, the daily communicants), just about sums up the situation.

If only they could be disabused of this hateful notion that they may not communicate except just after confession! If they all realized that they were perfectly free to receive the holy Eucharist (mortal sin apart) and that God wants them to do so, would they not crowd up to the Communion rails? If they truly understood that their act of worship was incomplete without Communion, would they not accept it?

Apply this, now, to yourself. I am presuming that you are a practicing Catholic who comes to Mass every Sunday. Well, suppose you are there and that you have not broken your fast (for that is the present law. It was not always so, and perhaps the time may come when again it will not be so. But that is how the law stands now).[2] The bell rings for the *"Domine non sum dignus"* and some people approach the altar rails. You have to decide whether you will leave your place and join them.

How do you decide? What question do you ask yourself? Do you ask, "When was my last confession?" That is the wrong question—it is off the point. The question which matters is, "Am I in mortal sin?" If the answer to this were to be "Yes!" (as I hope, is never the case), then of course you would have to stay in your place. You could not communicate. But if the answer is "No! not as far as I am aware"—then leave your place and go to the altar rails.

"But," you may say, "I haven't been to confession for a month! And I'm afraid I have committed all sorts of sins in that month. Surely I am not worthy to receive Communion?"

No doubt you have committed some sins during that month —owing to our human weakness we all do. But unless any of those sins were mortal sins, they are no obstacle to your Communion. As venial sins they were probably washed away by the "sacramental" of your taking holy water devoutly as you entered the church, or by your joining contritely in the *"Con-*

---

[2] Since the above was written the fasting regulations have been mitigated by the Apostolic Constitution *Christus Dominus* of Jan. 1953.

fiteor" at the beginning of Mass. You may have committed them indeed, but their guilt is no longer with you and they should not hold you back.

And of course you are not worthy—who is? All that matters at the moment is that you *qualify* by reason of *not* being in the state of mortal sin. You have the life of grace in your soul. You are a living member of the Mystical Body. Therefore you are invited by God to partake of the sacrificial gift you have just offered to Him.

And you should heed His invitation whether your last confession was last week or last month or last year . . . the length of time since your last confession is not the point at all. It is *grace* which is, at this moment, the point that matters.

So you see, confession is not necessary every Saturday as a condition of receiving holy Communion every Sunday. If it were, the Communion would be a burden, since a whole lot of people who can and do get to Mass each Sunday just cannot get to confession each Saturday. And it is a thousand pities if they think that that debars them from weekly Communion.

That many do so think I am absolutely convinced. This wrong idea holds incalculable numbers of Catholics from weekly Communion. They think weekly Communion means weekly confession—and that is more than they can tackle. They can (and do) manage confession periodically—say, once a month; but they then *limit* their Communions to those Masses which immediately follow their confession. At the intervening Masses they do not communicate; and the reason is not that they have fallen into mortal sin, but simply and solely the fact that they have not just been to confession.

What harm this idea does to souls! How it reduces the nourishment of the Mystical Body of Christ, and spoils the completeness of the sacrificial worship offered by so many!

Please note carefully that I am not trying to discourage frequent—even weekly—confession. If people want to confess weekly, by all means let them do so. The Popes have in recent years made a special point of encouraging frequent confession. What I am denouncing is the idea that this is *necessary* in order to receive holy Communion.

And I denounce it because it is not the truth; it is contrary to the teaching of the Church and is responsible for the omission of holy Communion at Mass by untold numbers of Catholics who could communicate.

So think very seriously of what you do if you omit to receive Communion as part of your Mass. You behave in a way which is both unnatural and ungrateful. You spoil things.[3] For, if you are doing your offertory properly, and taking part as you should in the canon, you are, in effect, saying to God: "Dear Lord, I love You! And I want to make You a present!" "What present?" says God. "This bread and wine, Lord! This means me. I gave You my whole self under this symbol at the offertory; and now I am joining myself to the perfect Gift: the sacrificial body and blood of Your beloved Son." "Thank you," says God; "I am very pleased with that. And to show that I love you too, I am going to give you a present in return." "What present, Lord?" you ask. "This same holy Bread!" replies God. "Receive this body of My beloved Son, for your spiritual nourishment now, and as a preparation for eternal life." And if you do not accept It when you might, you are answering, in effect, "No, thank You, Lord. Not today, thank You. I am not taking Your present. I prefer to do without. Some other day perhaps . . . some other time . . . next week, maybe; or next month. But not now. I shall get on without Your present."

Can that be pleasing to God? Is that the right and natural and reasonable way to treat God? Yet that, in practice, is the answer of those who come to Mass and yet, though not in mortal sin, do not "partake from this altar of the most sacred body and blood" of God's Son.

[3] I am abstracting, of course, from cases where individuals find it impossible to come to Mass fasting, even according to the new fasting laws.

Discussion Questions

1. How is it natural that there should be a preliminary *exchange of words* in Mass before the *exchange of gifts?*
2. What is the meaning of the *exchange of words* in the Fore-Mass?
3. Describe the *exchange of gifts* in the Mass from the Offertory on.
4. Do you think there could be a better way to exchange words and gifts than the Mass, one personally more pleasing to you or to God?
5. Discuss the question: Should all those at Mass receive Holy Communion?
6. Describe how the frequency of receiving Communion at Mass has varied in the history of the Church.
7. What forms of apathy and ignorance about Communion are common now? Are they as widespread in your parish as Father Howell implies they are generally?
8. Would being at a party at a friend's house on Saturday night, or going to a movie, etc., make you unworthy of receiving Communion on Sunday?
9. What is wrong with connecting Communion with confession in our thinking rather than with the Mass?
10. We consider a neighbor to be conceited if he refuses every friendly offer of assistance. When we neglect Communion are not we, spiritually undernourished as we know we are, telling God, "No thanks, I don't want your help"?

CHAPTER FIVE

THE MASS IS A LITURGY

ACTIVE PARTICIPATION

SUPPOSE A RICH MAN builds a hospital, staffs it with doctors and nurses, and then no sick people ever go to it. What's the use of it? It does the people no good. The work of that rich man needs their co-operation if it is to profit them. Suppose another rich man builds a great library and fills it with thousands of wonderful books—only to find that nobody ever goes there to consult those books. What's the use of it? It would be sheer waste of money and effort. If it is to be any use to anybody, then people must use it. It needs the co-operation of the people if it is to profit them.

In an earlier chapter we saw that such actions of public benefactors like these were once called "liturgies"; and these men were called "liturgists." But after a while these words were restricted in their meaning to designate only men and

The picture. A liturgy is a religious act which requires the co-operation of all concerned. In the picture, men, women and children (all the faithful, in the side-panels) adore and praise and thank God in the Eucharist (which means "thanksgiving") by joining in the song (woman) or the music of instruments (man with harp) or the gestures (children waving branches) through and with the priest (center) in the great Sacrifice of the Mass which all offer together.

actions of this type done by them in the *religious* sphere. A "liturgist" came to mean some man who did something that had to do with religion—something which, though done by him, was done for others, and which needed the collaboration of those others if it were to have any effect. The religious action thus done was called a "liturgy."

And we saw also that the greatest liturgy ever done was the saving and sanctifying work of Christ our Lord; for though this was done by Him, He did it for others (for us); and it needs the collaboration of those others (that is, of us) if it is to have its effect. Christ is the Great Liturgist.

He first did His liturgy at a particular date in history; and He did it through the instrumentality of His physical body. But He continues it throughout all time "in mystery," carrying it on now through the instrumentality of His Mystical Body.

But it is still liturgy; and so it still requires the collaboration of those on behalf of whom it is done.

That means us; for it is for us that our Great Liturgist now continues His liturgy, just as it was for us that He did it in the first instance.

"The sacred liturgy," says the Pope, "is the public worship which our Redeemer, the Head of the Church, renders to the heavenly Father, and which the society of Christ's faithful renders to its founder, and through Him, to the eternal Father" *(Mediator Dei,* n. 20). Which is the same as saying that "the public worship which the Redeemer . . . and the society of Christ's faithful render to the eternal Father *is liturgy."*

The public worship, therefore, requires the collaboration of those who worship. They must *do something*—they must *take their part* in the liturgy. "The faithful assemble in church," wrote Pope Saint Pius X, "for no other object than that of acquiring the true Christian spirit from its primary and indispensable source, which is active participation in the most holy mysteries and in the public and solemn prayer of the Church."[1]

[1] *Motu Proprio* of 1903, obtainable from the Gregorian Institute of America, 2130-32 Jefferson Avenue, Toledo 2, Ohio.

Now of all these holy mysteries the sacrifice of the Mass is the chief. It is the supreme worship of the Mystical Body in general, and of that body of the faithful in particular who, on any given occasion, are there to offer the Mass at a given altar. It is the worship of a *community*.

This is the point I want to emphasize now. It is one act of worship by a *body* of people; it is not, therefore, a mere sum of the individual acts of worship of a lot of individual people who happen to be present in the same church at the same time.

To see this difference, imagine that you enter a church to make a visit to the Blessed Sacrament. Two other people are also making visits. You notice a third person saying the rosary at our Lady's shrine; a fourth is praying before the statue of St. Joseph; a fifth is moving quietly and devoutly around the stations of the cross; a sixth is outside the confessional making preparation for, or thanksgiving after, confession.

All these people are worshiping simultaneously and in the same church. But nobody would dream of asserting that they are worshiping as a *community*. They are—very rightly and properly—busy with their private devotions as *individuals;* and the mere fact that they are all praying in the same church at the same time does not turn their private devotions into community worship.

What, then, is community worship? It is worship which derives its communal nature not merely from the fact that a number of people are present at the same time, but from some other factor which unifies these individuals *into* a community. This factor is the co-ordination of their activities (which still themselves may be diverse) into one predetermined pattern having one intrinsic and specific purpose.

Neither the pattern nor the purpose is determined by these people; both pre-exist; but they are accepted and appropriated by these people who voluntarily co-ordinate their own (possibly varied) activities into that pattern, directing their minds and wills to that one purpose which specifies the pattern.

An example might be public rosary. In that, not only are all the people present together, but all are saying the same words and thinking the same thoughts at the same time. In this instance, however, there is no diversity of activity.

Contrast this with "May Crowning" of the statue of our Lady when different people do different things. Some walk in procession; some carry the crown; one puts the crown on; others sing predetermined hymns or pray specified prayers. But these different activities all contribute to one pattern which those present did not themselves determine, but which they all do accept and appropriate by voluntarily co-ordinating their own activities for the one purpose—the honoring of our Lady—which specifies the ceremony as a whole. This "May Crowning" is a communal act—that is, *one thing*—just as much as a public rosary is one thing, even though different people have different parts to play.

Now the Mass, because it is by its essence community worship, is likewise *one thing*. It is offered by many indeed, and among these there is diversity of activity (as in May Crowning); but its *oneness* depends on the co-ordination of diverse activities into one predetermined pattern having one intrinsic specific purpose. It is *one thing,* just as a drama is one thing or an opera is one thing.

Within the unity of an opera there are many different people having different activities. There may be a hero, a heroine, some lesser characters, and a chorus; there will be a conductor and an orchestra, a stage manager and scene-shifters. Each has something to do—his own part; and this is not the same as somebody else's part but is a "set part" predetermined for him, designed to contribute to the unity of the whole.

The actors and singers cannot themselves decide what notes or words they will utter; the members of the orchestra cannot decide for themselves what tunes they will play. If everybody sang or played just what he liked whenever he liked and how he liked, then the result would not be an opera but an uproar.

So also in the Mass there are a lot of people with their own parts. At solemn high Mass there is the priest as the principal human minister without whose specific activity there would be no Mass at all. But also there are the deacon, the subdeacon, the acolytes, the thurifer; there is the choirmaster and his choir and maybe an organist; and there is the "community of Christ's faithful." Each of these has a set part to do, which contributes to the whole and completes its unity. If anybody does not do the prescribed part, or does just whatever he likes, this spoils the whole.

And the pity of it is that nowadays there is nearly always something which does spoil the whole—somebody not doing the prescribed part but doing instead something different, according to his own preference.

Those who are in the sanctuary normally do their parts well enough. But when it comes to the choir's part and the people's part there is frequently disorder. The choir have got certain parts which belong to them; these are the choir's business and consist of the introit, gradual, offertory verse and communion verse. The choir's job is to sing these at the proper times. Yet many choirs tend to shirk them. Either they leave them out (which is absolutely forbidden by the Church's laws) or else they recite them in a perfunctory manner on one note, or just to a psalm-tone, instead of using their skill and musicianship to sing those parts to their own proper music. Choirs don't seem to want to do their own job.

And the people? They, too, have their own parts. These are the responses, and the *Kyrie, Gloria, Credo, Sanctus* and *Agnus Dei*. All these are people's parts and *not choir's* parts. The people should sing them. Yet so often they just won't. They sit there absolutely dumb and do precisely nothing. Not a chirp out of them. The priest greets the people by turning to them and singing *"Dominus vobiscum"*—but the people pointedly ignore him. Their only rejoinder is stony silence. Though, of course, they don't mean it that way, the fact is that their behavior is, objectively, rude in the extreme. So the choir make the reply instead.

And the same goes for the other people's parts—*Kyrie,*

Gloria, Credo, Sanctus and *Agnus Dei*. The people who should sing them remain dumb. So the choir take them over. And often, instead of treating them as prayers to be sung for God's glory, they treat them as operatic choruses to be sung for the entertainment of themselves and of the people. They turn the church of God into a concert hall; they use the Mass as a background for the display of their virtuosity as a kind of sacred glee-club. Yet the Mass is supposed to be sacrificial worship, and not a concert.

The reforms so long needed in this matter were begun by the Pope Saint Pius X in the *Motu Proprio* of 1903 which I have already quoted. It is a long document with many precise instructions, but what it all amounts to is that these performances by sacred glee-clubs to congregations of aphonic dumb-mutes ought to stop, and both choir and people ought to do their own jobs and do them properly.

Of course the Pope expressed it more politely than that, but hardly less emphatically. "We do therefore publish, *motu proprio* and with certain knowledge, Our present instruction . . . and with the fulness of Our Apostolic Authority do give it the force of law, and by Our present hand-writing We impose its scrupulous observance on all. . . . These things We command, declare and sanction, decreeing that this Apostolic Constitution be now and in future firm, valid and efficacious, that it obtain full and complete effect, all things to the contrary notwithstanding."

That is what Pope Saint Pius X ordered fifty years ago. But as for its "full and complete effect" . . . that is hardly more visible than its "scrupulous observance!" Someone (I think it was Fr. Gerald Ellard, S.J.) has said that this is the most evaded and ignored decree ever issued by the Apostolic See. How right he is!

All that is about high Mass. But all is not well with low Mass either. Low Mass is just a simplified form of high Mass with the music left out, and the priest speaking the prayers of the absent deacon, subdeacon and choir. But there are still *people* at low Mass, and their parts remain. But normally they get done by a small boy while the people do nothing.

The practice is fortunately growing whereby the people all say their parts instead of leaving them to the server. This is called "dialogue Mass" and is certainly a step in the right direction. Various forms of it have been approved by many bishops, both in the United States and in many other countries. It should be encouraged in every possible way, and the people should join in as heartily as they can. Because all this helps to make the Mass, even in its outward form, correspond to its inward reality, namely, communal worship.

Priests who want their people to take their own part—whether by singing at high Mass or by reciting the answers at low Mass—often get mighty little co-operation from their people. In fact, they meet with a whole lot of opposition. That is so because many people have no idea of the Mass as a "liturgy." They have the wrong spirit—the individualist spirit—instead of the collaborative and communal spirit which should be that of members of the Mystical Body of Christ.

Such people are unwilling to coordinate their own activities into the predetermined pattern which constitutes the Mass as an act of communal worship. Instead they "want to say their own prayers." Which shows how little they understand the Mass or their position as members of the Mystical Body.

Once upon a time the whole of Europe was Catholic. Everybody believed *not* what he pleased, but what the Church taught. Everybody accepted *not* a moral code of his own choosing, but what the Church declared to be right or wrong. And everybody worshiped God *not* according to individual fancy but (at least in public worship) in the way the Church desired and arranged. Then, in the course of time, there came abuses and revolts and finally schism and heresy; Protestantism arose, tearing whole nations from the unity of the Church.

The fundamental principle of Protestantism is what is called "the principle of private judgment." Protestants say a man has a right to decide for himself what he will believe; he can choose this or that religion just as he thinks fit. They object to the Catholic Church "dictating" what is true or false, what is right or wrong. That is why they reject the Catholic Church—they "protest" against it. They say they will believe, they will behave, and they will worship as they think fit, not as somebody tells them. The "principle of private judgment" is the very essence of Protestantism.

Of course not everybody became Protestant; the majority of European Catholics, in fact, remained true to the Church. They rejected this principle of private judgment and continued to accept the guidance of God's Church in matters of faith and of morals. The spirit of Protestantism—the principle of private judgment—did not undermine their creed or their code.

But it did have *some* effect. It affected their cult—their worship. Gradually—surrounded as they were by Protestants with this spirit of private judgment by the individual—Catholics became infected with this spirit in the sphere of their worship. They began to worship not in the Church's way—communally, as a body, co-ordinating their activities into the Church's pattern, all doing their own proper parts—but rather "in their own way," each individual exercising private judgment about what he would do at public worship.

And that spirit of individualism has descended even to our own day. We still find enormous numbers of Catholics who will not worship communally as the Church desires, but who, during public worship itself, "prefer to say their own prayers."

This very Protestant attitude is often found most deeply rooted in seemingly very "pious" Catholics. They "like to say their own prayers"; they won't join in the Mass. They won't sing at high Mass and they won't answer at dialogue Mass. They say "it distracts them from their prayers." Yet they ought not, during *public* worship, to be at *"their* prayers"; they ought to be giving their minds and hearts to the *community's* prayers—to the Mass.

But they won't; they exercise their private judgment as to

THE MASS IS A LITURGY

what pleases *them;* instead of joining in with those parts which the Church allots to them, they "say their own prayers."

And the result is fantastic. In an opera, various people have various things to sing, but all those things are prescribed for them by the composer—they are not what they choose for themselves. All those things are designed to fit together to make one intelligible whole. Now suppose somebody came to the front of the stage and began singing "The Star-Spangled Banner" while somebody else went to the right and began singing "Dixie"; at the same time somebody is at the left singing "Jingle Bells" while a fourth person is at the back of the stage singing "I've been wukkin' on de Railroad!" (or "O Lady of Fatima!" which has largely the same tune).

Would you call that an opera? Of course not—it would be confusion and nonsense. People singing what they want, when they want and how they want instead of singing their own parts designed for them by the composer!

But something very like that so often happens at Mass. The priest is putting the meaning into the gifts at the offertory. The composer of this work—the Church—means him to have a sort of supporting chorus of the people all putting *their* meanings into the gifts. But that doesn't happen. Mr. A. doesn't join in that. He "prefers to say his own prayers." He likes "The Thirty Days Prayer" and gets on with it. Mrs. B. won't join in either—she is making a novena to St. Sacharina. Mr. C. prefers something that doesn't involve any trouble—he says a lot of "Hail Mary's." Mrs. D. is a very devout soul . . . she likes to feel good, and immerses herself in a most touching meditation book she has discovered. It is called "The Heart Throbs of the Languishing Spouse for Her Celestial Lover."

The net result is a travesty of what the Mass should be—it is a riot of individualism, a fantasy of the Protestant spirit of private judgment, everybody doing just what he or she likes instead of doing what the Church desires as a contribution to that unified and communal action which is the Mass. One wonders whatever almighty God makes of it all!

What should they be doing? The Pope makes it clear enough in *Mediator Dei:*

"They must not be content to take part in the eucharistic Sacrifice by the general intention which all members of Christ and children of the Church must have; they ought also, in the spirit of the liturgy, to unite themselves closely and of set purpose with the High Priest and His minister on earth" (n. 104).

"To unite themselves closely and of set purpose" means that they ought to tell God they are sorry for their sins when the priest tells God he is sorry for his sins; they should cry for God's mercy when the priest cries for God's mercy; they should praise God when the priest praises God; they should listen to God's word when the priest announces God's word to them; they should put the meaning into the gifts when the priest puts meaning into the gifts; they should believe and wonder and admire when the priest, by the power of God, turns the gifts into the Victim of Calvary; they should offer this divine Victim to the Father when the great High Priest and His human minister are offering the divine Victim; they should receive the return-gift of God when the priest receives the return-gift of God.

That is what they should do. They should do it by singing their parts when singing is to be done; or, at low Mass, by speaking their parts when these are to be spoken, or expressing themselves in their own words or in words from a suitable prayerbook or in the Church's own words from the best book of all—the missal. Those are the things they should be doing in order to "unite themselves closely and of set purpose" with communal action.

Wherefore they should not be praying to our Lady when God's message is being announced to them; they should not be praying to St. Anthony when the priest is putting the meaning into the gifts; they should not be making a novena to St. Maria Goretti when the priest is offering the Victim; they should not be praying for the souls in purgatory when the priest is receiving or distributing the return-gift of the sacrifice.

Behaving like that brings confusion and disorder into the unity of the act of worship; it turns it from the communal action which it ought to be into the simultaneous performance of a lot of disparate individual devotions. All the things which these people are doing may be good in themselves; it is good to pray to our Lady, to the saints, and for the souls in purgatory. But these private prayers should be done in private time, not during the public celebration of the community-sacrifice.

If only people saw the unreasonableness of these practices, if only they would forego their personal preferences for the communal good and the glory of God, then the Protestant spirit of private judgment would be replaced by the "true Christian spirit" of which "active participation in the most holy mysteries" is the "primary and indispensable source." Then those priests who "strive to make the liturgy a sacred action in which, externally also, all who are present really take a part" *(Mediator Dei,* n. 105), would meet with less opposition when they exhort their people to sing at high Mass or respond at dialogue Mass.

And then "if this be happily brought about, there will no longer be any need to lament the sad spectacle in which the people do not respond at all, or only in a subdued and indistinct murmur."[2] And there would be some prospect that the Mass will become in fact that which it is in theory—namely, the communal offering of all members of the Mystical Body, united in mind and will, to the honor and glory of God.

[2]Pius XI, *Divini Cultus,* 1929.

Discussion Questions

1. Why is it natural that the Mass-liturgy should require our collaboration?
2. What is the difference between a community and a collection of individuals? Defend the claim that Mass is the worship of a *community,* not of a sum of individuals.

3. A working girl has different accomplishments to offer to God in Mass than a grade-school child has. Discuss the way in which every person should unite his or her individual offering with the action of the Mass so that it is part of *community* worship.
4. Pope Pius X reminded the Christian world that singing also belongs to the people's part in worship. What prayers and responses in a high Mass should the people sing, and why? What are the obstacles to congregational singing of the Mass?
5. A play or an opera is one performance because all the parts follow a pre-determined pattern having one intrinsic and specific purpose. In the Mass-opera it is Christ, of course, who determines the pattern and purpose, and the priest who does the visible directing. What are the sentiments of liturgical piety that the people as a kind of chorus should express as the Mass progresses?
6. Discuss the effect of the "principle of private judgment" on the people's participation in the Mass.
7. In what ways could we cooperate with our pastor to achieve greater community worship?
8. Discuss ways of bringing more Catholics to *want* to participate in Mass as a communal action.

All - Honour and - Glory

CHAPTER SIX

PROBLEMS OF PARTICIPATION

THROUGHOUT PART I of this book, and in the first five chapters of Part II, I have been attempting to give an elementary explanation of the main principles and doctrines involved in the Church's liturgy. I have addressed myself in imagination to "beginners"—people who are new to the "liturgical point of view." And my first purpose was to give them a new angle on the practice of their religion in the Mass and the sacraments. But a second purpose was to help other readers who, though they really knew about these things before reading the book, were nevertheless seeking for illustrations and ways of expounding them to others.

With the discussion of the Mass as "a liturgy," as one unified action of a sacrificing community, I believe I have covered all the main points needing treatment for the fulfillment of those two purposes. Wherefore I might very well stop here and write no more, considering my task as completed.

But there is something I want to add; it is something mainly directed to the second class of readers, and yet I hope and believe that those of the first class will be able to follow it.

The picture. It is by their active participation that the faithful give "All honour and glory" to God (triangle; YAHWEH) through Him (Christ: Eucharistic species) and with Him and in Him.

For if they have absorbed the viewpoints expounded so far, they are, at this stage, no longer mere "beginners."

That which I desire to add concerns what is known as the "liturgical movement." This is the sum total of the efforts made by all those who have learned to understand the spiritual riches of the liturgy in their attempts to bring that same understanding to others. They desire that God be worshiped as perfectly as possible by all the members of Christ's Mystical Body; and they want all these members to be enriched as much as possible by the graces which flow from Christ the Head of the Body.

Now the liturgy itself is the means to both of these ends; for by the liturgy God is worshiped, and through the liturgy the souls of men are enriched with grace.

The liturgical movement, therefore, is concerned directly with fundamentals—the glory of God and the sanctification of man. It is not directly concerned with externals, such as the style of vestments, the beauties of Gregorian chant, the dignity of ceremonies, and so forth. But it has to be concerned with them *in*directly, because it is these things which give shape to the liturgy *through which* God is glorified and man is sanctified.

The "practical liturgist"—he who is actually striving to bring men to God by means of the liturgy—cannot evade preoccupation with these things, even though they be not in themselves his ultimate objective. They are, however, his tools; so he must understand them and know how to use them.

He uses them in the pursuit of the first practical objective of the liturgical movement—that which was enunciated in the famous words of Pope St. Pius X: "the primary and indispensable source of the true Christian spirit is the *active participation* of the faithful in the holy Mysteries and in the public and solemn prayers of the Church."[1]

In other words, the first practical task of the liturgical movement is to get the people actively to participate in the liturgy.

[1] *Motu Proprio,* Nov. 22, 1903.

Without practice it is all theory; if the liturgical movement is to *move,* then things have to be *done.* Active participation is both "primary and indispensable."

Active participation might be internal (of the mind and will) or external (of the bodily powers—movement, senses, voice). It is the internal participation which is essential; if the mind and the will are active in worship, then the worship is genuine. If only the bodily powers were active—with no corresponding activity of the mind and will—then the result would not be worship but mere external ritualism.

The ideal participation involves both. For, as man consists of soul *and* body, activities of the soul tend naturally to express themselves externally. Thus, if a man is just bursting with happiness, he is likely to break forth into blithe song. But the converse also holds true; external activities tend to engender the corresponding internal dispositions. Thus, if a man who is feeling depressed joins in some cheerful song, he is likely to cheer up.

So the active participation sought for the liturgy is to be perfect—that is, it must be internal and *also* external. The external participation is needed because it is a means to the production of the internal participation aimed at as essential; and also because without it man is not wholly, but only partially engaged in his worship.

When the Pope speaks of active participation he is obviously including the external, for, in the *Motu proprio* from which the phrase is taken, his main subject is singing the Mass. And Pope Benedict XV, likewise demanding active participation, refers to "prayers, rites and chants";[2] Pope Pius XI says the people must not be as "dumb spectators" but that "their voices should alternate with those of the priest and choir."[3] Pope Pius XII approves "the efforts of those who want to make the liturgy a sacred action in which, *externally also,* all who are present may really take a part."[4]

[2]Benedict XV, Allocution, July 1915.
[3]Pius XI, Apostolic Constitution, Feb. 16, 1929.
[4]Pius XII, *Mediator Dei,* n. 105.

Many other quotations could be given to show that the words "active participation in the liturgy" mean, in the mind of all these popes, *external* active participation (of course conjoined with the essential internal dispositions). It is in that sense that I use the words henceforth.

The practical, immediate objective of the liturgical movement is, then, to cause people actively to participate in the liturgy, since this is a means towards the ultimate aim, the glory of God and the sanctification of man. But this practical objective is by no means easy to achieve—especially in the most important of all liturgical functions, which is the Mass. There is a very serious problem to be faced, and it is that problem which I desire to discuss now in these final chapters. For nobody can work intelligently towards a goal if he is merely aware that "there are difficulties." He has to see precisely what those difficulties are, and what causes them, before he can do any effective work to overcome them.

Why, then, is it so difficult to get the people actively to participate in the Mass? What are the causes which operate to produce their present state of inactivity? In the previous chapter I imputed blame to the people themselves. But that is only half the picture; there is another side to it too, and it is that which we must now examine. The fact is that there is some excuse for the people. The liturgy of the Mass as we have it now, and have had it for many centuries, is such that the great majority of our Catholic people experience serious difficulties if they desire active participation, external as well as internal.

And the solution does not lie in mere instruction, for the amount of instruction that would be needed is greater than is feasible. What they would need for the present Mass-liturgy is more than instruction—it is education; education, moreover, up to a standard which they are not normally likely to get. It is within the grasp of but a small proportion of the Christian people as a whole. Is it right that the Sacrifice of the whole Christian community should be enacted in a manner which is proportioned to a mere few? Should not genuine active participation in the sacrifice of all be within the powers of all? Yet it is not.

This problem actually arose many centuries ago; the fact that it has not been solved has cost the Church dear. It was not even properly diagnosed until Pope St. Pius X pointed out that "the primary and indispensable source of the true Christian spirit is *active participation* in the solemn and public worship of the Church." But so long as the public and solemn worship of the Church is presented in a form such that the people cannot fully participate in it, then they are insofar cut off from the primary and indispensable source of the true Christian spirit.

This is the heart of the whole problem—a disparity between *what* the Mass really is, and *how* the Mass is celebrated. For the Mass is, according to its intrinsic essence, community worship. Yet the external form in which that worship is now embodied is such that the communities who are supposed to worship in that way find it largely beyond their powers to do so. The external form of the Church's public worship, such as it is now normally celebrated, does not seem to suit the Church as a whole; it suits rather a small cultured minority of the Church. All the rest are restricted to a greater or lesser degree of passive spectatorship; the external form of the Mass—which in fact is their Mass just as much as anybody else's Mass—is alien to their minds and dispositions.

In other words the present Mass liturgy, though venerable from long usage, though filled with treasures of doctrine and devotion and beauty and art which are the delight of cultured people, is not fully functional as the vehicle of community worship of the "toiling masses."

And the trouble lies not only in the existence of this state of affairs, but in the inability (or unwillingness?) of cultured people to see it and face up to it. Many of them so value the esthetic excellencies of the present Mass-liturgy that they cannot reconcile themselves to any proposals for liturgical reform which would diminish these esthetic excellencies, even if such reforms would bring the liturgy within the reach of those who have a right to understand and participate in it—namely, the common people.

Let us study the problem more closely. The principal act of Catholic worship is the Mass. And the Mass is by its nature, which no externals can alter, the sacrifice of the Church. For, as Pius XII says in *Mediator Dei,* "Every time the priest re-enacts what the divine Redeemer did at the Last Supper, the sacrifice is really accomplished; and this sacrifice, always and everywhere, necessarily and of its very nature, has a public and social character. . . . This is so, whether the faithful are present . . . or whether they are absent" *(Mediator Dei,* n. 96).

No merely external circumstances, therefore, can alter the intrinsic nature of the Mass. "Every time the priest re-enacts what the divine Redeemer did at the Last Supper," whether this be done in Latin or Greek or Hebrew or Glagolithic, audibly or inaudibly, in speech or in song, with people present or absent, active or inactive, vocal or dumb, the underlying reality of the Mass remains ever the same. The Mass is the sacrifice of Christ's Mystical Body, the Church, and its social and public character is inseparable from itself.

But it should be obvious that this social and public character, though it can never cease to exist, is capable of varying degrees of manifestation. What Christ did at the Last Supper may be re-enacted in a way which shows forth its public and social character; or it may be re-enacted in a way which conceals or disguises its public and social character. In other words it is possible for its external form to manifest (and thus correspond with) its internal nature; and it is possible for its external form to conceal (and thus be out of harmony with) its internal nature.

And though it does not make any difference to the Mass itself, it does make an enormous difference to the faithful whether the public and social character of the Mass is expressed or not. For if it is so expressed to them, then they can understand that it *is* public and social worship and that they can publicly and socially participate in it. But if the public and social nature of the Mass is hidden in its externals, then they do not perceive its public and social nature, do not understand it, and cannot participate in it except with difficulty.

Moreover, if the externals of the Mass—that is to say, its liturgical form—do express the internal reality of its social nature, then the form fits the content. It is something genuine, vital, "in order." Whereas if the Mass-liturgy obscures the internal reality of its social nature, then the form does not fit the content: it is something alien, disordered.

And the problem of public worship has arisen precisely because the Mass-liturgy, which was designed to express its public and social nature (and once actually did so), no longer does so adequately. Once it was a fitting and living vehicle of public worship; but now it might be compared to a beautiful museum piece which expresses all too little to our people. It obscures from them the underlying reality of the Mass and renders their active participation in it so difficult that normally they take no external part in its liturgy at all.

As Donald Attwater wrote (*Orate Fratres,* October, 1936): "The practical expression of our religion and its activities which we call liturgy is cast in forms entirely foreign to the civilization of today; we offer forms of public worship to people whose mental outlook and life make it almost impossible for them to worship in that way."

Or, as Fr. Paul Doncoeur, S.J., puts it (*Orate Fratres,* March, 1947): "A lifeless ritualism can smother all the religious life of our people. They cannot be sustained, they cannot continue to live, except by means of a liturgy which is life-giving, and which they can assimilate.... This is a very serious problem, a problem not only engaging the interest of scholars and esthetes, but one that should cause concern and anxiety to all who find themselves responsible for their people before God. For we see here a frightening application of the axiom: *Lex orandi, lex credendi*—the law of worship is the law of faith. If our worship is disordered, then our faith will be disordered;

if our liturgy is moribund, our faith will die too. This is a cry of alarm which I utter. For, alas, we must have the courage to admit that in some respects our liturgy is no longer vital; I mean, of course, not in its substance, but in its outward form. It is no longer vital among the people."

To see how vital it once was, and contrast it with things as they are now, let us reflect a little on the history of the Mass-liturgy.

What our Lord did at the Last Supper was simply this: He took bread and wine which His apostles had placed before Him; He turned these into His body as given and His blood as shed; and He distributed the results amongst them. So He instituted that which was, by its nature, a sacrifice; and by its form, a communal meal. And He told them to do the same in memory of Him.

Now this simple action of His became surrounded in time by a ritual; a ritual which was intended not merely to invest the proceedings with solemnity, but also to expand, to explain, to manifest ever more clearly all that was involved in these actions of our Lord. And this ritual in which His own actions became enshrined is what we call the liturgy of the Mass.

This differed in different times and places; but it is generally agreed that it attained particular excellence under Pope St. Gregory about the end of the sixth century. By revising forms in use under his predecessors he produced a ritual of actions and words which was admirably suited to the needs of his own flock—the Catholics of Rome. For them it was a living liturgy—easy, natural, intelligible—in the course of which they, as the Roman Christian community, prayed together, were instructed together, offered sacrifice together, and received of its fruits together.

Its external form perfectly expressed its underlying reality; it corresponded, that is to say, with the fact that this was the public and social offering of sacrifice by the Church.

We shall look at some of its details in the next chapter. But meanwhile think of the most common form of the Mass—the

Low Mass—as we have it today. Is it easy, natural, intelligible? Does it even look like social worship? Does it "expand, explain and manifest ever more clearly what was involved in the actions of our Lord" at the Last Supper? Have we not in fact reached a state of affairs wherein we have to take endless trouble to explain that which ought of itself to be an explanation? Just think it out!

Discussion Questions

1. What are the goals of the "liturgical movement"?
2. The sponge at a party—the fellow who is passive and *does nothing* to make the party a success—doesn't please the planning committee. Does this throw any light on why the liturgical movement insists on active participation of all the faithful in the Mass?
3. In what ways does external active participation inspire internal participation and thus serve the ultimate goals of liturgy—the glory of God and sanctification of man?
4. How does mere external ritualism differ from the genuine "active participation" in the liturgy which Pope Pius X called to our attention? Give examples of what appears to you to be mere ritualism.
5. If the Mass is community worship, its celebration should be adapted to active participation by the whole community. Discuss the present *facts* of participation as you know them. For example, only young boys are allowed to serve. What attitude might this imply?
6. It is a sad fact that relatively few people participate fully in the Sacrifice of the Mass. Father Howell finds the cause for this in the disparity between *what* the Mass really is and *how* it is celebrated. Discuss the problem of whether the public and social nature of the Mass has become too hidden in externals strange to our way of living.
7. Sometimes we look for a *fast* Mass so that we can get out *early*. We want to "get it out of the way." Are we really willing to take the time, do the studying, etc., to increase our participation? Do we want to spend as much time and energy preparing for Mass as we do for weekly golfing or fishing or club parties?
8. How should Sunday Mass carry over into our daily living until the next Mass in which we participate? By the way we offer it? By its sanctifying effects? By the spirit of our prayer during the week?
9. Should working people and busy housewives look forward to sharing in occasional weekday Masses?

CHAPTER SEVEN

A GLANCE INTO THE PAST

IN APOSTOLIC TIMES the Mass must have been very simple. We do not know many details except that it began as "evening Mass" and was done at the end of a supper for which the Christians used to meet together. But after a while it got transferred to the end of another type of meeting in the morning at which they had prayers, sang psalms, and read the Scriptures. By the middle of the second century the Mass-form had clearly emerged as what we would call a "General Meeting" of all the Christians of any one place. The community was headed by its bishop, whose relationship to his people was something like that of a pastor these days; he had just a few priests and deacons to help him, and these few were his entire

The picture. Here we see Holy Mother Church displaying her two tables of sacred nourishment. On one is the Eucharist, the Bread of Life. But Christ said: "Not by bread alone does man live, but by every word that comes forth from the mouth of God." Hence on the other table we see the Bible, the Word of God. It is at Mass that Mother Church ministers both of these to her children. First she breaks for them the Bread of the Word (Epistle, Gospel, sermon), and then she breaks for them the sacred Bread of everlasting life (sacrificial meal). Thus in two senses we may say that the Mass is "The Breaking of Bread."

clergy. In fact, a primitive diocese was in many ways rather like a parish of today.

The bishop presided at the weekly Mass-meeting from a throne behind the altar, with his clergy seated on each side of him. The altar was not against the back wall, nor had it any tabernacle. Mass began with Scripture readings, which the bishop explained in his sermon. Then, as described by St. Justin about 150 A.D., "bread and the chalice with wine and water are brought to the president of the brethren; he takes them, gives praise and glory to the Father in the name of the Son and of the Holy Ghost, and gives thanks at length for all the gifts we have received from Him. When he has finished the prayers and thanksgiving, the whole crowd standing by cries out in agreement: 'Amen.' . . . After the president has given thanks and the people have joined in, the deacons distribute to all present the bread and the wine-and-water mixed, over which the prayer of thanksgiving has been offered."[1] When you recall that the technical term for a "prayer of thanksgiving" is a "eucharistic prayer," you will see here the clear outlines of Offertory, Canon and Communion.

This sort of thing used to be done every Sunday by bishops all over Christendom. They did it in the language of the people—Aramaic, Syriac, Greek, or whatever it might happen to be in that place. (But not, at first, in Latin! That did not come in till there were Christians who talked Latin, about the middle of the third century). The bishop made up the prayers as he went along, and the precise form of words did not matter so long as he stuck to the point, which was to thank God for His gifts and tell (and do again) what our Lord did at the Last Supper. But after a while certain forms of words became customary. Some of the prayers even got written down. Thus there grew various "local liturgies." Things went on like this until the sixth century.

About the end of that century there came a very great Pope,

---

[1] St. Justin. "First Apologia" ch. 65.

St. Gregory. He made a collection of the prayers and customs in vogue throughout the Western (now Latin-speaking) Church, and from this material he fashioned a liturgy for his own diocese of Rome. He did not impose it on other bishops; but what he compiled was so good that others began to copy it, and it ended by spreading gradually all over the West.

This liturgy shaped by St. Gregory was built up according to certain principles which had been at work in all the Mass-forms of all the local churches from the earliest times. His title to glory rests on the fact that he applied these well-known principles more fittingly, more artistically, more effectively than had any other bishop elsewhere.

The first principle was the use, in worship, of the selfsame language which the people used in their everyday life. The earliest Roman Christians were predominantly of the Greek slave class; their language was Greek; and so Greek was used both in their instruction and in their worship. In the course of a few generations their children "lost the Greek" and took to the Latin of those among whom they lived, just as Germans or Italians who emigrate to America usually begin by talking their own tongue but fail to preserve it beyond their children or their children's children.

When Greek was no longer spoken by the faithful in Rome, it was no longer used in their worship. Instead, the prayers and instructions were in the tongue they now used in their daily lives, namely, in popular Latin. Not, you will note, in the classical literary Latin of the cultured classes, but in the Latin of the people. That, then, was the first principle of the Roman liturgy of St. Gregory's time—the use of the vernacular.

The second principle, enunciated long before by Pope St. Clement I, was what we might call "differentiation of function." In the body there are many members, but not all the members have the same function. So also the Mystical Body of Christ in its worship has many members, but not all have the same function. Some are to do one thing, some another.

"We must do in an orderly fashion," he wrote, "all that the

Master appointed us to do. He commanded us to celebrate sacrifices ... which we should do thoughtfully and in due order. For to the presiding priest his own proper liturgy is appointed; to the priests a proper place has been assigned, and the layman is bound by the liturgy of the laity. Let each of us, therefore, brethren, make the Eucharist in his own proper order, not transgressing the fixed rule of each one's own liturgy."[2]

The second principle is, then, that the various things to be done by the community at worship should be apportioned among various people; all were to do their own parts, fulfilling their own functions, not taking to themselves the functions of others. The celebration was to be hierarchic—in due order.

According to these two principles, and making use of prayer-forms customary even before his time in Rome, Pope St. Gregory put together the most perfect Mass-liturgy that has ever existed. It is worth our while to review its main features.

To begin with, the Christian community were to have communal prayers, instruction and song. Hence:

(1) *The Entrance Rite.* The sacred ministers entered, accompanied by the song of the people led by the schola (group of trained singers). The celebrant, having entered, greeted the people and prayed in their name. (Introit and collect.)

(2) *The Instruction.* There were Scripture readings, variable in number and interspersed with psalm-singing. These readings were given by different officials, *not* the celebrant. The last was the deacon, who sang the gospel. After these readings the celebrant gave the homily. (Epistle, gospel, sermon.)

Now the community proceeded to offer sacrifice. Wherefore:

(1) There was the offertory procession, in which the people brought their gifts to the altar, singing a psalm as they came. The celebrant chanted (of course aloud, and in their own tongue) a prayer over the gifts. (Offertory, secret.)

(2) Next came the Eucharistic Prayer, in the course of which the people's gifts were transformed into the Victim of Calvary,

[2]St. Clement's *Epistle to the Corinthians,* chap. 41.

and offered in sacrifice to God. This, of course, was the celebrant's own special part; but the people had some share in it at the beginning (preface responses), in the middle *(Sanctus* chant) and at the end (the "Great Amen"); and they had the function of being witnesses throughout, since it was all chanted aloud in their own tongue so that they heard and understood every word of it.

(3) The community, having given their gift to God, now approached to receive God's return-gift, by partaking of the sacrificial Victim from the altar. This Communion procession was preceded by the singing of the Lord's Prayer and the Breaking of Bread, accompanied by the people's own psalm-singing, and followed by the final prayer of the celebrant and dismissal by the deacon. *(Pater Noster, Pax,* Communion, post-communion, *Ite.)* And that was all.

In this wonderfully simple and crystal-clear Roman Mass-liturgy there are several points worthy of our special attention, because it is precisely the lack of these which makes our present Mass-liturgy difficult from the standpoint of the people's participation.

(a) There were no private prayers of any kind; every word of the whole ceremony was audible to the people; every word, being in their own tongue, was intelligible to them.

(b) Every part was actually done by those to whom it was assigned; nobody did anybody else's part—each "made the Eucharist in his own proper order, not transgressing the fixed rule of each one's own liturgy."

(c) The intrinsic purpose of each phase of the Mass-drama was not only obvious, but was actually achieved.

In these three respects the present Mass-liturgy offers a startling contrast. As regards point (a), there are many "private" prayers (e.g., *Aufer a nobis, Suscipe Sancte Pater,* secret, Canon, pre-Communion prayers) which the people do not hear at all, and would not understand if they did hear them (because in an unknown tongue).

As regards (b), the people's parts are constantly being taken over by the choir at a sung Mass, or by an altar boy at a low Mass. And the priest does everybody's parts as well as his own; he does introit, gradual, offertory and communion, which belong to the choir; he does epistle and gospel, which belong to the other ministers; he does *Gloria* and *Credo* and *Sanctus,* which belong to the people.

As regards (c), the intrinsic purpose of, for instance, the introit, is not in the least obvious. It is meant to put appropriate thoughts into the minds of the community, but in fact it usually does no such thing; it seems to be just "incidental music" by the choir. It is by no means obvious that the readings are to instruct the people, since those who sing or read them turn their backs on the people and use an unknown tongue. And the people are not in fact instructed by these actions. It is not very obvious that the offertory is the presentation and hallowing of the people's gifts, for the people see little, and hear and do nothing. (In this case, however, the intrinsic purpose *is* achieved—as also in the Canon.)

Probably the most serious drawback of the modern Mass-liturgy is that indicated in point (b)—the complete eclipse of "differentiation of function." For it was this, above all, which made apparent the social nature of the sacrifice. Now that the priest does everything, the result looks like a "one-man sacrifice"; and this, after all, is precisely what it is *not.*

This liturgy of St. Gregory's was very obviously social; it was something of great interest, intelligible from beginning to end, moving, inspiring, and at certain points even spectacular. And it was all entirely practicable, within the capabilities of the common people. They did not have to learn any dead language; they did not have to be taught how to use missals; they did not even have to be able to read. Only the sacred ministers and the schola had to have that much culture. The common people were able to take their full part in the liturgy equipped with only those powers which pertained to them as human beings—namely, the power to see, to hear, to walk, and to sing.

But alas, this wonderful, living, fascinating **Mass-liturgy**, within the capabilities and grasp of the entire Christian community, did not survive St. Gregory's time by much more than a century or two. The people were gradually reduced to that role of "silent and detached spectators" which all but the cultured have today. How did this happen?

There were all sorts of factors at work throughout the course of many centuries. It is impossible here to do more than sketch out just a few of them.

Missionaries went forth from Rome, taking Gregory's Massbooks with them. They came to countries where Latin was not spoken, where local languages were often primitive and undeveloped. Some of them, like SS. Cyril and Methodius, observed the Roman principle that the language of worship should be the language of the people, and so they fashioned a liturgy in the tongue of their converts. Hence the Slavic liturgy which is still with us today.

Others, however, did not make similar adjustments. They preached, indeed, in the local vernaculars so far as they could learn them—they had to, for otherwise they could not have taught the people at all. But when it came to worship, they stuck to the familiar Latin because they had gotten used to it. This was the way they had always done it—and they went on doing it. This meant that the common people could not take part in the singing, except for a few simple easily-learned phrases like *"Et cum spiritu tuo"* and *"Amen."* The psalm-singing during the four processions at the entrance, gospel, offertory and Communion had to be done by those few whom the missionaries were able specially to train in the singing of Latin psalms.

This had two unfortunate results. Firstly, the people lost their own function of being a sort of "general chorus" with an important part in the liturgy; they were reduced to the status of being listeners, merely "represented" by the schola. Secondly, as time went on, these scholae became ever more expert at singing. Being now unimpeded by the musical limitations of the common people, they began to develop their hitherto simple chants into elaborate compositions filled with florid neums.[3]

By the ninth century things had got a stage further. Musicians were now singing so many notes per syllable that they took a long time to get through their appointed texts. As a result the celebrant was often kept waiting. At the offertory, for instance, he was ready to sing his prayer over the gifts long before the choir had finished. Hence some private prayers, said by the priest inaudibly, were put in to fill up his time and keep him suitably occupied. This principle of inaudible prayers being once admitted led to the prayer over the oblations being likewise said inaudibly. Only the end phrase was kept out loud because it had to be answered.

Likewise the *Sanctus* chant had become so complicated that neither priest (unless he happened to be a musician) nor people could sing it. Hence the choir sang, the people kept silent, and the priest *said* it in a low voice. Then, instead of waiting till the choir had finished, and singing the Canon aloud, the clergy got on with it silently before the choir had got through all their neums. As the people could not now understand the Latin Canon anyway, what matter if they could not hear it?[4] The silent Canon and all the interpolated silent private prayers in due course found their way back to Rome itself—probably through travelling monks and returning missionaries.

For by that time even in Rome itself the people's language was no longer Latin; it was Latin in process of developing into Italian. And in other civilized parts of the Roman empire the once common Latin was developing into what we now call French, Spanish, and Portuguese. The common people everywhere ceased to understand the Latin liturgy which was now

[3]Cf. Ellard, *Mass of the Future,* chap. 8.
[4]In the course of time, arguments were thought up to justify this, especially the idea that for reasons of reverence the Canon must be hidden from the laity. Cf. Ellard, *op. cit.,* chap. 11.

within the grasp only of the clergy, the monks, and the educated nobility.

Hence the people ceased to love the Mass as it deserves to be loved, for they could neither understand it nor take part in it. They came with diminished frequency; and they rarely communicated, especially as the offertory procession dropped out through the use of unleavened bread, and money-collections were introduced instead.[5] The liturgy, like its language, threatened to become a dead thing among the people. Moreover low Masses became increasingly common, and were promoted by reason of the stipends attached to them.[6] Sung Masses became ever less frequent until they were hardly to be found outside monasteries and cathedrals.

Thus gradually, over the course of centuries, the living, organically active and united worship of clergy and people together became a sort of formal ritualism, the almost exclusive preserve of clerics and religious. All that the people could do was to watch. And even that became less interesting when the priests turned their backs to the people, removed the altars from their proximity, and built great screens which cut off the choir (clergy's part) from the nave (people's part) of the churches. The poor folk then could not even see.

The active external participation of the people was thus gradually hindered by these changes in the sung Mass; and the same holds true, to an even greater degree, of the developments in *low* Mass. It was here that the principle of "differentiation of function" died too. There being no deacon, no subdeacon and no choir, the priest took over the functions of them all. He did everything, whether it was really his business or not. And the practice of the celebrant reading introit, epistle, gradual, offertory and Communion found its way ultimately into the sung Mass as well.

All these changes were in the sixteenth century incorporated into rubrics which have perpetuated them to this very day.

[5] Cf. Ellard, *op. cit.*, chap. 9,
[6] Cf. Ellard, *op. cit.*, chap. 7.

Perhaps it is not to be wondered at that the people, having been deprived of playing their full, active role in the Mass, grew very ignorant about it, and almost never communicated until the Fourth Council of the Lateran, in 1215, made the law that all *must* communicate at least once a year. It is small wonder also that ignorance and apathy became so widespread that there flourished all those manifold abuses which finally contributed to the great upheaval and revolt of the mis-called Reformation. We cannot by any means put the sole blame for the Reformation onto the "reformers."

In the chaos of those evil days it was, of course, absolutely necessary that the Mass be rigidly stabilized by a measure of reform and the imposition of hard-and-fast rubrics, even though modern research into liturgical history has shown that some of these are ill founded. One shudders to think what might have happened to the Mass later on it if had not been so strictly controlled. Look what occurred later to those externals which were not so minutely regulated—the music and the vestments. The music degenerated into mere "Grand Opera"; and the vestments, especially the chasuble, have suffered lamentable distortion. Certainly we may be glad that the Mass itself became stabilized by such inflexible rubrics; this very fact has preserved it until modern scholarship was in a position to solve many problems.

But one feels that now, after four centuries, when the danger of the Protestant Reformation has passed, and there is a new awakening to the greatness of the Mass, a reform of rubrics in the light of subsequent liturgical research is urgently needed. For, as they are, they constitute one of the major problems of the practical liturgist who is working to restore active participation of the people. These rubrics were made in the days when there was no participation by the people whatever. And as their purpose was to *keep* the Mass as it then was, they tend to keep it such that the people cannot participate actively now.

That is why at present we have to resort to all sorts of partial expedients which are liturgically unsatisfactory, such as making somebody read the epistle and gospel in English *while* the priest reads them in Latin. These expedients are not "the real thing"; they are activities in the nave which merely run parallel with the activities in the sanctuary—they are not integrated into the liturgy itself. It is not *one* thing which is going on, but two.

However, there is good reason for hope. The new Holy Saturday rubrics, for instance, do give us "the real thing" in the congregational candle-lighting and in the vernacular renewal of the baptismal vows. We should be duly grateful—and not cease to pray for more such reforms. In time, please God, we shall have them. But until we do have them we have to admit that there are serious reasons which make it difficult for the people to behave otherwise than as "silent and detached spectators." Our present liturgy, as I have endeavored to show, is not truly a people's liturgy but a liturgy for the cultured.[7] May the intercession of Pope St. Pius X, who so desired "active participation of the people," advance the solution of this urgent problem.

In the meantime, however, we may not rest content with sitting back and doing nothing, while "waiting for reform."

[7] To quote Fr. Doncoeur again: "This liturgy of the Church is not and never can be other than the liturgy of all the people. It cannot be the worship of single individuals or of a favored group. I make exception here of the monastic liturgy which is the worship of a community culturally and spiritually select. But the *parish* liturgy—and it is that alone which concerns us here—cannot be other than the worship of the whole community of all the people. It must be 'popular'; it cannot be reserved to an elite, not even to an elite which is culturally more advanced. . . . It is the action of the entire Mystical Body, and the entire Mystical Body should share in it. . . . If we are thinking only of persons who possess a certain degree of culture, and who are therefore able to enjoy certain forms of expression, then we no longer speak of liturgy for the people— nor even of the liturgy altogether. I should not hesitate to employ the phrase 'liturgical snobbery,' for we would be yielding to a detestable aristocratism if here, when it is a question of souls, we ignored the great body of the faithful in favor of a privileged class." This whole article, in *Orate Fratres*, March 1947, is deserving of very earnest study.

All available expedients must be tried, within the framework of existing laws, to achieve whatever degree of active participation is here and now possible. And for this purpose the experience of the liturgical movement, of thousands of zealous clergy and tens of thousands of devout laity, must be called upon for help and guidance. Despite present handicaps, much, very much, can be attained when there is good will and love of proper divine worship.

Books and pamphlets, many of them excellent, furthering an intelligent appreciation of the Mass, are multiplying. With personal effort we can always increase our internal participation, and carry out the consequences in terms of community spirit and fraternal charity. However historical developments may have affected the celebration of the holy Sacrifice, the fact (and obligation) remains that "the Mass is the chief act of divine worship; it should also be the source and center of Christian piety" *(Mediator Dei,* n. 201).

In other words, in given instances, there may be an excuse for "silent," but never for "detached spectators."

Discussion Questions

1. Describe the simple action and spontaneous prayer of Holy Mass in the first Christian century as we know it from St. Justin's writings.
2. In the early centuries of the Church the principle that public worship should be in the language of the people was taken for granted. Discuss the pros and cons of using the vernacular at the present time.
3. Pope St. Clement wrote (c. 190): "Let us make the Eucharist, each in his own proper order according to the role appointed for his liturgy." Comment on the importance of this principle of "differentiation of function" for understanding the social nature of the Eucharist.
4. On the principles of vernacular and diversity of function Pope St. Gregory I developed a classical Mass-liturgy. Outline the stages of its action.
5. In what striking ways does this early Mass-drama contrast with ours?

6. Discuss the historical conditions (introduction of private prayers, keeping a language unknown to the people, failure of the people to carry out their own functions) which lessened the active participation of St. Gregory's time.
7. Discuss the advantages and disadvantages of the imposition of inflexible rubrics which took place in reaction to the Reformation. What changes in the rubrics would likely increase active participation?
8. What "expedients" have been and could be used to restore more active participation by *all* the people?
9. Have you participated in the new Easter liturgy for Holy Saturday? If so, how did it provide more active participation?

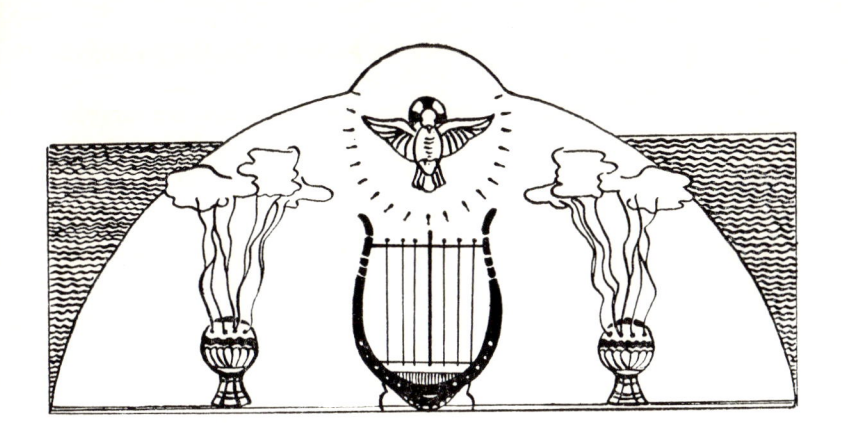

CHAPTER EIGHT

LITURGICAL PIETY

THE DIFFICULTIES in the way of the people's participation, which were discussed in the previous chapter, were the external difficulties arising from the present form of the liturgy. But this failure of the external form of the Mass to express to the people its internal content has given rise to a very serious *internal* difficulty which also needs to be studied.

It is the fact that their minds are not attuned to the social nature which is intrinsic to the Mass. They are individualists, whereas the Mass is in reality community worship. Hence the true nature of the Mass is alien to their dispositions. Their personal piety is not in harmony with the action that is going on; hence not only are they, in general, unable to take part, but they are not willing to take part, even to the extent which remains (though with difficulty) open to them.

This is because their piety is not derived from the "primary and indispensable source" which is "active participation in the

---

The picture. The Church of God in her liturgy is ceaselessly carrying out the task described by St. Paul to the Ephesians: "Be ye filled with thy Holy Spirit (Dove), your tongues unloosed in psalms and hymns and spiritual music (lyre) as you sing and give praise to the Lord (incense)."

liturgy." It is derived from secondary sources which are largely individualistic devotions. It is these which shape their minds. The liturgy, because it has become for them a dead thing, exercises no influence in forming their attitude.

It was not always so. In early days the people understood the liturgy (for it was in their own tongue) and took their full part in it (for it was constituted of elements which were all within their natural powers of seeing, hearing, walking and singing). The liturgy was, in consequence, something which had a profound effect on their mental and spiritual formation. It was a "live thing"; it gripped their attention and welded them together in conscious unity; it made them active in praying, singing, giving and receiving, in constant union with the sacred ministers and with each other. It brought to them no sense of loneliness, no repression, no aloofness; there was no sense of compulsion, of mystification, of irrelevance or of boredom.

Rather there was fascination, joy, enthusiasm and inspiration. And all of this engendered in them a certain spiritual attitude or "type of piety" which was based on vivid realization of those basic truths which the understood words and participated actions of the liturgy constantly impressed on them.

They vividly realized and powerfully felt that these basic truths intimately concerned themselves. They might not have been able to express them in the accurate terminology found in our modern catechisms; but these truths meant far more to them than they do to our modern people.

What are these fundamentals which the liturgy of those days, year in and year out, so effectively brought home to them, and which therefore conditioned and orientated their whole spiritual outlook?

It is clear from many early writings that have come down to us, especially from the way in which their preachers talked to them, that these early Christians were filled with the spirit of joy. They exulted in the conviction that Christ their Lord had liberated them from the death of sin and endowed them with His grace; they triumphed in the knowledge of His victory over the devil; they gloried in the consciousness that He was their Head, the First-born of many brethren. They knew that they were themselves the brethren, belonging to each other in one body with Christ.

To them Christ was the one Mediator through whom they had access with confidence to their heavenly Father. They were elated in the assurance that through Him and with Him and in Him they could offer to God the Father all honor and glory. For them the whole of life was a Godward movement made possible for them by the fact that their triumphant and risen Lord, who had Himself gone to the Father, had made them His very own. He was now reigning in glory at the right hand of the Father, and one day He would come again in majesty to summon them into His eternal kingdom. He had conquered sin and death, and given to them grace and life. They felt all this as concerning themselves because they were members of His Body which is the Church.

For Christ, then, they lived; in Christ they would die, so that through Christ they might rise again to eternal life with the Father.

These are the thoughts which are constantly expressed in the liturgy; these are the truths which penetrated their minds by reason of their habitual participation in the liturgy; these are the convictions which shaped their outlook and formed their attitude towards their religion.

Their piety thus was a communal piety, motivated by their incorporation into the Church, the Mystical Body of Christ. Their piety was Christo-centric, ever concerned with Christ their Savior, their Head, their Mediator. Their piety was joyous and triumphant, in the spirit of the "Gospel" or Good Tidings that they were redeemed, baptized, endowed with grace and destined for everlasting life.

How different things became when people became estranged from the liturgy by reason of the fact that they could no longer participate in it or understand it! By the Middle Ages the liturgy had not changed with the people and so it became an exclusively clerical ritual in which the people had no part. They could but watch with unperceiving eyes and listen with uncomprehending ears. They were no longer spiritually nourished by intelligent and active participation in communal sacrifice; the great basic truths living in the liturgy did not take possession of their minds and shape their attitude towards life.

Hence the piety inspired by the liturgy practically died out. A very different type of piety began to grow and develop.

Whereas in olden days there had been a communal or gregarious sort of piety based on the communal cult of the Church, inspired by the consciousness of grace, of membership of the Mystical Body, and centered on Christ the Mediator, now there arose instead an individualistic type of piety, man-centered, concerned with the salvation of the individual soul, with the fear of sin, the consciousness of guilt, and the need for intercession. The spirit of joy was largely taken out of religion, and the spirit of fear took its place. There arose that cultual dread, that sense of unworthiness in the presence of "the awful mysteries" which was the forerunner of Jansenism.

The concept of the Church as a living organism of the grace-filled brethren and members of Christ became obscured, and uppermost in consciousness was the view of the Church as a juridic organization with power to impose commands under pain of mortal sin.

Instead of thinking of themselves as "the saints," as "God's chosen people, holy and well beloved," the faithful regarded themselves as dreadful sinners hanging over the pit of hell. Preoccupation with personal salvation and its difficulties through sin evoked a kind of spiritual covetousness for indulgences; awe of the Godhead of Christ pushed His mediatorship into the background of consciousness, so that the people turned increasingly to secondary mediators who could more easily be approached because they were but human—the Mother of Christ and the saints. It is, of course, perfectly right to pray to our Lady and the saints; the Church herself teaches us to do so; but not to the extent that places any of them in the center of devotional life. This most important and central position belongs only to Christ Himself.

"Devotions" of all kinds arose—the only ways in which the people could now exercise their piety, seeing that they had little outlet in the Mass itself. As the great dogmatic truths and their immediate relevance became less apparent to the popular mind, there was an increasing dispersion of effort in spheres which are merely peripheral to the redemptive and sanctifying work of Christ.

An enhanced value was placed on arousing personal *feelings*—feelings of contrition, of sorrow, of compassion, of pity, of love. Piety became measured largely by the intensity of personal emotions which its various exercises engendered; devotions were assessed in proportion to the favors they were reputed to obtain. A lack of balance and dogmatic soundness became ever more apparent in the expressions of popular piety.

Of course the people still knew the great truths; they knew that Christ had redeemed them on His cross, that He had risen and ascended into heaven, that He had conquered sin and death; but they believed these things with a kind of notional assent, much as we might believe that Julius Caesar once conquered Gaul.

These were not the considerations which colored their minds and motivated their worship. They were concerned rather with avoiding sin, escaping hell, winning merits, curtailing purgatory, obtaining favors and so forth. It was an attitude utterly different from the joyful, communal, Christo-centric outlook of the early Christians.

And this is the heritage from which the piety of our modern peoples is descended. Apart from that small minority who have been touched by the recent liturgical revival, our people live and move and have their being in this spiritual atmosphere so divorced from the liturgy. They are nourished almost exclusively on private devotions, which they carry on even *during* liturgical functions, instead of entering into the thought and action of those functions.

Most of these private devotions have a spirit which is quite different from that of the liturgy. The prayers which they offer are largely pre-occupied with self, with petitions for personal favours, with endless protestations of personal unworthiness and a great deal of sentimentality which strains after emotional effects. They are full of "Oh's" and "Ah's" and words like "ineffable," "vouchsafe," "have recourse"; devout people are made to describe themselves as "miserable abandoned wretches," as "hanging over the pit of hell," as "filled with ingratitude," and in many other ways conflicting with the fact that they are "God's chosen people, holy and well-beloved," members of the Mystical Body, brothers and sisters of Christ, heirs to heaven.

The conclusion, of course, is *not* that practices of devotion other than the liturgy should be discouraged. Most certainly they have their legitimate place (though this is not *during* liturgical functions). But they should not have a greater nor even an equal formative influence on the popular mind as compared with the liturgy itself. They ought not to have a style and content which *unfits* people psychologically for due participation in the liturgy. Instead they should, as Pius XII says, "be influenced by the spirit and principles of the liturgy" *(Mediator Dei,* n. 184). They should be such that they "strengthen the spiritual life of Christians and *help them to take their part* with better dispositions in the august sacrifice of the altar" *(op. cit.,* n. 35).

A spirituality which is formed only by private devotions, and not at all by the liturgy, is ill-balanced; it is the cause of the abuse, so widespread these days, that the people carry on with their *private* devotions (legitimate in private time) *during* the *public* and social worship of the Mystical Body of Christ.

The liturgy is used as a sort of "holy background" for the entirely different personal devotions of a lot of people who are simultaneously present, but are not disposed to take any part in corporate worship. They just do not want to do so, for any such activity would "distract them from their prayers."

This I hold to be the key problem of public worship as it faces us today. The *ex*trinsic difficulties of the esoteric liturgy we have had for centuries have produced an *in*trinsic difficulty of mental maladjustment.

The only radical cure for this is a reorientation of the public mind from their hyper-sentimental, individualistic, self-centered type of piety to the dogma-filled, communal and Christocentric type of piety which is enshrined (or should one say buried?) in the liturgy. If they are to worship liturgically, then they must learn to think and feel liturgically. For otherwise they would be performing external actions which are not expressive of their internal dispositions. This would be mere empty ritual, since the ultimate purpose of such actions is none other than to express the interior acts of the mind and will.

The complete solution to the problem is to form the people's minds *by means of* the liturgy. There ought to be a Mass-liturgy which will of itself grip their interest, delight their minds, warm their hearts, evoke their cooperation and give them scope for joyful, intelligent and enthusiastic participation. Such a liturgy would of itself instruct them, form their minds, move their wills and expand their hearts, thus producing a type of piety in conformity with itself.

I am convinced that it will have to come some day, though naturally we cannot expect it just yet. Changes would have to be made very gradually, to give the people time to adapt themselves. It would not be possible, nor would it be desirable, to restore in modern times the identical Mass liturgy which St. Gregory designed for the people of his own day. But what is needed is something which would suit our people as well as his Mass liturgy suited his people; and before that can be devised there will have to be a lot of research and controlled experiment.

What, then, can be done in the meantime? We shall have to be content with partial and local solutions. Our goal must be to bring to the people as full an understanding of the present liturgy of the Mass and sacraments as may be possible with things as they are.

We must keep them in touch with the Church's liturgical year by such expedients as getting them to sing, before and after Mass, vernacular hymns suited to the feast or season; we must draw them into the activity of the worship by teaching them to sing the responses and the common (to simple settings) at high Mass, and to answer the responses (dialogue) at low Mass; we must utilize lectors to read the epistle and gospel at such Masses; we must devise token offertory processions, well-ordered Communion processions, and all those other ways and means which practical liturgists have thought out as being feasible yet not in conflict with existing rubrics.[1]

But most important is the psychological preparation which must precede these practical steps. If we cannot form the people's minds *by* the liturgy which is in Latin that they cannot understand, then we must try to form them *for* the liturgy by instructions in the vernacular which they can understand.

We must, as Pius XII says, "see that they are instructed concerning the treasures of devotion which the liturgy contains, by sermons, and especially by dissertations, periodical courses and Weeks devoted to the study of the liturgy" *(Mediator Dei,* n. 202). According to canon law every parish must have a mission periodically. One could wish for some law that every parish should, every year, have one "week devoted to the study of the liturgy."[2] Unless some such practice becomes generally adopted, no real progress will be made.

It is certainly possible—though as the fruit of much hard

---

[1] This paragraph, written in 1952, has now been vindicated by the Instruction of the Sacred Congregation of Rites in 1958. Apart from offertory processions (which the Instruction does not mention, as its subject is vocal and instrumental participation in the liturgy), all the other suggestions are provided for and recommended.

[2] It is to meet this need that I devised "Layfolks' Week," which instructs the laity, by a method of active participation in material selected from the liturgy, concerning their dignities, privileges and functions in the liturgy.

LITURGICAL PIETY

work—to make a proportion of the people in any given parish take *some* active part even in the present liturgy. But this will do little or no good, and can have no permanent results, unless the people are helped to understand what they are expected to do and why they should do it. Their minds must first be formed to appreciate it, to accept it, and thus to collaborate.

In other words, the basic elements of liturgical piety must be instilled into their minds (even if these do not take possession of their minds as fully as they would do if imparted by the liturgy itself rather than by mere instruction *about* the liturgy). It takes a lot of preliminary work to achieve any lasting success in the liturgical apostolate of a parish. But we can be encouraged by the fact that many priests, working on these sound lines, have achieved a great deal. In America there are a number of parishes where the people have been admirably trained and led to a high degree of intelligent participation in the liturgy. As the influence of the liturgical movement increases we may hope for many more such model parishes. And there are heartening signs that all these problems are being closely studied by experts with the encouragement of the Holy Father; there can be no doubt that he is eager to continue the liturgical reforms already begun in the restored Paschal Vigil, the new Psalter, the granting of vernacular Ritual, of evening Mass, of mitigation of the Eucharistic fast and several other ways. He will grant us other fruitful reforms as and when he judges that the time is ripe.

The very minimum mental equipment which people need before they can be said to be "liturgically minded" would be, I think:

(a) Some realization of the true nature of the supernatural.

(b) Some grasp of the Mystical Body doctrine.

(c) A clear view of the mediatorship or priesthood of Christ.

(d) Some understanding of their own share in this priesthood.

(e) An apprehension of sacrifice as the supreme act of worship.

(f) An appreciation of corporate worship.

All these ideas have been discussed in the preceding chapters. I hope, then, that they may be judged to have served their purpose as an introduction to the subject of liturgy for those to whom such viewpoints were new, and as a teaching aid to those whose concern it is to pass on these ideas to others.

But I would like to emphasize that they are but an introduction. There is an immense sphere of fascinating interest waiting now to be explored by those who will take the trouble to follow up this mere beginning by further reading in the many more advanced books and periodicals which deal with "liturgy" under its various aspects.

"May the God we worship graciously grant to us all that with one mind and heart we may so take part in the sacred liturgy during our earthly exile that it may be a preparation and prophetic token of that heavenly liturgy wherein, as we trust, together with her who is the august Mother of God and our most dear Mother, we shall one day sing: 'Blessing and honor and glory and power, through endless ages, to Him who sits on the throne, and to the Lamb'" *(Mediator Dei, n. 209).*

Discussion Questions

1. How much does the average Catholic look upon "private" spiritual devotions as religious acts entirely separated from the Mass? Do we tend to place greater "importance" and confidence in private devotions than in the Mass?
2. Worship necessarily reflects and builds up a certain way of looking at life. What in the liturgy of the early Christians gave them their joyous sense of triumph with Christ?
3. Compare the social and joyous sentiments of active participation which should be present in offering Mass with the generally prevalent piety of Catholics at Sunday Mass.
4. What changes in the people's understanding of the Church caused liturgical piety to give way to individualism in the Middle Ages?

5. At the consecration a lady is busy lighting a votive candle before a statue. Is modern piety self-centered by comparison with the Christ-centered outlook of the early Christians?
6. Discuss the possible unbalanced emphasis of many of our modern devotions during Mass.
7. Discuss Father Howell's claim that our individualistic piety is a direct result of a liturgy too foreign in appeal to inspire and form a joyous Christ-centered worship.
8. What criterion does Father Howell set up for judging the quality of private devotions as "to style and content"?
9. What concrete steps can be taken in the typical American parish to help the faithful develop a wholesome piety by means of the liturgy?
10. What workable steps can you formulate for your own group to advance the liturgical apostolate?
11. State in brief form the fundamental truths which Catholics must *appreciate* before they can worship liturgically?

SELECTED TITLES FROM THE POPULAR LITURGICAL LIBRARY

THE WEEK WITH CHRIST
Liturgy for the Apostolate
EMERIC LAWRENCE, O.S.B.

Conceived as a companion-book to the Sunday Missal, this volume has become popular with lay readers as a very effective means for bringing the liturgy of the Sunday Mass into the home and making it an everyday Christianizing influence of American life. It is both modern and streamlined, the meditation material being stripped of religious-life techniques for the more simplified needs of working men and women. —*The Ave Maria*

CHRIST ACTS THROUGH SACRAMENTS
A. M. ROGUET, O.P.

"With the modern re-emphasis upon the doctrine of the Mystical Body and the union of Christ with Christians, theologians have been delving into the problem of causality of Christ's mysteries upon the souls of the faithful, and the connection between the mysteries and the sacraments and the effect they produce. The author broaches his discussion with the statement: the sacraments are the acts of Christ. The style is terse and the thought presentation is sometimes elliptic. The book furnishes excellent material for study groups. —*Catholic Review Service*

GOD'S WORD AND WORK
The Message of the Old Testament Historical Books
KATHRYN SULLIVAN, R.S.C.J.

For several years now, Mother Kathryn Sullivan has been assisting the readers of WORSHIP to rediscover the treasures of the Bible. The publication of these valuable essays in a single volume will bring an even wider reading public to appreciate the depths of Old Testament spirituality. The theme of the book, the *mirabilia Dei,* God's continued acts of mercy and redemption on behalf of his Chosen People, is a precious key to a proper appreciation of the Old Testament. In Mother Sullivan's capable hands, it becomes an instrument that is managed with great dexterity and utter simplicity. With admirable self-denial, she has concealed her profound erudition, marshalling all her literary skill to the one aim of bringing to the contemporary Christian the ancient yet ever-new message of Israel's salvation-history.—David M. Stanley, S.J., *Professor of Sacred Scripture,* Jesuit Seminary, Toronto, Canada.

HOLY WEEK AND EASTER
JEAN GAILLARD, O.S.B.

We are, indeed, grateful to the author, Dom Jean Gaillard, for this commentary on the liturgy of Holy Week and the Easter octave, in which he places the Easter Vigil in its immediate setting and thus brings out the fulness of its meaning and purpose.

In a series of meditations on the sacred events of these days the author combines historical information and spiritual inspiration. He lays great stress upon the Easter Vigil service as a personal and community experience of our sharing in the risen life of Our Lord through the graces of Baptism and the Eucharist.

We owe a debt of gratitude to the Reverend William Busch for bringing this commentary to the American public by his excellent translation. —*in the book's* Foreward

THE CHURCH'S YEAR OF GRACE
DR. PIUS PARSCH

"Holy Mother Church teaches and all learn. But we can learn only insofar as our minds are open. Father Parsch's work is an ideal vehicle for opening our minds to the words of the teaching Church. . . ." —*Altar and Home*

A SHORT BREVIARY

"It would be most natural for any person who has become accustomed to using the missal at Mass to desire to go a step further. "A Short Breviary" makes this step possible . . . Men and women, no matter what their profession, should be able to include these prayers in their daily schedule. The compensation derived will far exceed the effort." —*The Tablet*

PREPARING FOR EASTER
REV. CLIFFORD HOWELL, S.J.

"Drawing upon his pastoral experience and his rare pedagogical talents, Father Howell has arranged a series of Lenten sermons in which the sublime mysteries of the Holy Night Liturgy are unfolded with a clarity and simplicity as to make them understandable to our lay people. No pastor, or assistant (or Catholic) should be without *PREPARING FOR EASTER,* which provides such valuable instruction for the people and such needed inspiration for the priests. Religious superiors, also, who give conferences to their subjects will find this booklet most helpful.

—*Social Justice Review*

Write for complete catalog.

POPULAR LITURGICAL LIBRARY
PACKAGE PLAN

All the following 100 widely used liturgical publications for
$5.00

HOLY MASS
- Our Mass
- The Funeral Mass
- Mass Symbols
- Study the Mass
- Why the Mass?
- Manner of Serving Low Mass
- The Masses of Holy Week
- The Chrism Mass of Holy Thursday

THE SACRAMENTS
- Rite of Baptism
- The Eucharist
- The Seal of the Spirit
- Christian Married Love
- Rite for Marriage
- Holy Marriage
- Last Rites for the Sick

GREGORIAN CHANT
- Parish Kyriale
- Six Chant Masses
- Marian Anthems
- Advent Song
- Lenten Song
- "Te Deum" in English
- Mass VIII (De Angelis)

DIVINE OFFICE
- Daily Prime
- Daily Compline
- Sunday Compline
- Praying the Psalms
- The Breviary and the Laity

SACRAMENTALS
- The Way of the Cross
- O Saving Victim
- Sisters' Way of the Cross
- Blessing of Children
- Family Prayers
- Family Life in Christ
- Family Advent Customs
- Lent and Holy Week in the Home
- Liturgy's Inner Beauty
- Sanctifying Pregnancy
- A Brief History of Liturgy
- Mixing Your Marriage?
- Novena to the Holy Spirit
- Madonna of the Americas
- Complete Set of Abbey Prints (60 designs)
- Selected Imported and Domestic Holy Pictures

Due to difficulties of maintaining stock, it may become impossible at times to include a title listed above.

100 items for $5.00

THE LITURGICAL PRESS
Collegeville, Minnesota